'A must-read for every executive who wants to stay sharp, up to date and on top of their game to tackle challenges and build their competitive edge. The 12 principles are well-rounded inspirational nuggets laid down in a way to ease personal upgrade or transformation. A great read indeed!'
   – Moira Homan, Human Resources Director, Podravka (Croatia)

'*The Performance Advantage* is not just recommended – it's essential. This book goes beyond being a mere guide – it becomes a catalyst for personal growth and transformative leadership. With every page, it challenges you to push your limits and unlock your full potential.'
   – Heidi van Eldik, Vice President Retail, Engineering &
      Manufacturing Benelux, DHL Supply Chain, Benelux & Nordics
      (The Netherlands)

'"I took matters into my own hands" is the quote that sums it all up: aspirational. The book has it all – honesty that draws you in from its first lines, tangible compassion and energy that radiates. That, all knitted together by practical advice, made it a read impossible to put down once you begin. Taking this book to read may be a critical step to take the matter into your own hands.'
   – Dr Karina Nersesyan, Deputy Regional Director, UNFPA Arab
      States (Egypt)

'I enjoyed the perspective that to be a high performer is a personal, active choice with trade-offs and requires constant reflection. Simple, practical takeaways on how to do this make it a very actionable book.'
   – Jon Talbot, Senior Vice President HR Executive Leadership,
      Deutsche Telekom (UK)

'In *The Performance Advantage*, Agnes embarks on an exciting leadership journey, guiding us through a dynamic set of 12 potent principles for the masters of high-performance leadership. The journey, filled with infectious motivation, hands-on tips and reflective moments, is a beckoning call to anyone seeking excellence and the curiosity to unlock the vault of high-performance thinking.'
  – Patrick van Weerelt, senior official, international organisation (Bonn)

'Honest, humble and empathetic, with a unique lens on the insights needed to challenge yourself to think and be better; Agnes manages to capture the essence of her wisdom and share it in a practical and structured way, anchored in what she has learnt as a leader herself, and from supporting leaders globally.'
  – Nick Heard, Chief Engagement Officer, National College of Education (UK)

'*The Performance Advantage* belongs on every bookshelf and deepens and lends a unique perspective to complementary classics in leadership and performance literature. The book is a quick read, and its chapters can serve as a go-to reference, worked through systematically alone, with teams or with a coach, or serve as a team resource or for coaching one's own staff.'
  – Dr Koko Warner, Director of Global Data Institute, IOM (Berlin)

'A power-packed, go-to guide for every leader serious about embodying excellence. In true Agnes style, full of inspiring guidance and practical tools throughout!'
  – Rachel Martino, Senior Manager, Honor (USA)

'This isn't just a book; it's an invitation onto a deeply inspiring journey. Agnes Cserhati possesses the extraordinary ability to help you elevate your thinking toward new heights. Some of the wisdom in this book is bound to stay with you for a lifetime.'
  – Annika Brack, CEO, International Centre for Future Generations (Brussels)

'Leadership is a journey, and my leadership journey has been transformed by Agnes's genius. Her 12 principles are truly life changing for any leader, and they give you the performance advantage.'
  – Dr Rose Mwebaza, Director and Regional Representative of Africa, UNEP (Kenya)

'The concept of performance advantage is transformational and deeply impactful. Agnes possesses a rare insight into the world of high performers. Her captivating leadership tales not only engage but also prompt reflection on one's own career and leadership journey.'
  – Julia Stone, Vice President of eCommerce and Digitalisation, telecommunications industry (Austria)

'Dive into this remarkable book for an extraordinary journey! Every chapter and every principle feels like an immersive coaching session on its own. With Agnes's wisdom and thought-provoking insights, it's the ultimate catalyst to elevate your leadership to new heights.'
  – Svitlana Bielushkina, People & Organisation Director for Digital Experience and Technology, Zalando SE, (Berlin)

'*The Performance Advantage* is a game-changing book that underscores the significance of determination and self-motivation in achieving goals. Challenging traditional leadership concepts, it spotlights the incremental shifts that lead to profound success. A must-read for those striving to break boundaries, tap into their full potential and script a remarkable journey to excellence.'
  – Dwiti Vikramaditya, Vice President KIIT & KISS University, MC/MPA Harvard Kennedy School 2023 and JFK Fellow (India)

'Prepare to be transformed. It is an unputdownable intellectual masterpiece. It is simply genius how Cserhati artfully navigates the readers to embrace the power of performance advantage.'
 – Ulas Hazar, Grammy-considered artist (Germany)

'A powerful, understandable and unique insight from a remarkable person. Agnes simplifies and breaks down critical and key performance areas in a way relatable to the ambitious striving to make their mark on the world.'
 – David Harkin, CEO, 8 Billion Ideas (UK)

'Super engaging and inspiring. Agnes's passion for leadership growth and exceptional performance jumps off the pages. In this book, she challenges and empowers you to become the best leader you can be and coaches you on this journey with her stories, experience and thought-provoking questions.'
 – Caroline Kersten, Talent Acceleration & Culture EMEA at a
   global life-science company (Switzerland)

'*The Performance Advantage* is authentic, practical and totally relevant for today's leaders and executives in our challenging and ever-changing world. Agnes shares the best of her experience as she leads you in transforming yourself and those around you!'
 – Nick Thayer, Corporate General Manager, insurance industry
   (Sydney)

'Wise and inspirational. An essential read for senior leaders! It empowers those operating at the highest levels in a very practical, specific yet adaptable way. It is time to experience the profound impact of PowerCoaching in a book, an approach from which countless global leaders and organisations have already gained value through coaching and training with Agnes.'
 – Thilo Kusch, Group CFO, P3 Logistic Parks (Prague)

THE PERFORMANCE ADVANTAGE

SUCCESS PRINCIPLES

12

Every senior leader needs
to know but executive
courses don't teach

AGNES CSERHATI

The Performance Advantage

ISBN 978-1-915483-31-7

eISBN 978-1-915483-32-4

Audio ISBN 978-1-915483-37-9

Published in 2024 by Right Book Press

A CIP record of this book is available from the British Library.

To all the exceptional leaders across the globe whose unwavering dedication and inspiring journeys have fuelled my own mission of 'sharing to inspire'. To Max and Dominik for their endless love and support. To my beloved grandparents, whose belief in me at an early age has been instrumental in shaping my path.

CONTENTS

INTRODUCTION

I was ten years old when I decided to be a high performer. As I sat at the back of my maths class on an ordinary Friday morning, feeling unchallenged and waiting for others to finish their work, my beloved grandfather's words echoed in my mind: 'Don't be afraid to stand out from the crowd but do not seek it.' In that moment, I understood that conforming to other people's expectations and blending in with the majority would not provide me with the opportunities I needed to learn, grow and reach my full potential. In the absence of external motivation and with a lack of interest from my teachers, I took matters into my own hands. I decided to challenge myself and embarked on a lifetime journey of pushing beyond the ordinary and expanding my comfort zone. I asked myself, 'Who understands, develops and challenges those who are successful and thriving? Surely they would also like to grow?'

Over the years, my fascination with human behaviour, leadership and self-development has deepened. I've relentlessly studied what distinguishes high performers from everyone else, what fuels their drive and how they unleash their untapped potential. I've personally experienced the sense of isolation and need for self-reliance that typically accompany such a journey. I couldn't bear watching untapped leadership potential go astray or remain unfulfilled at the highest levels. So I became committed to transforming this reality by empowering high performers to think differently about their leadership and careers.

Throughout my long career as a performance coach, leadership trainer and public speaker, I've had the privilege of working with a diverse group of top leaders, teams and organisations who span more than a hundred countries. Drawing upon this wealth of experience, I've cultivated a unique perspective that challenges conventional notions of performance, leadership and success. While I remain committed to my journey as a lifelong learner, I believe that the time is right to share with you my 12 PRINCIPLES of high-performance success, which have already benefited so many. Now it's your turn to elevate your leadership and take your career to the next level.

Leadership is a journey to be embraced, a journey of privilege, responsibility, growth and courage. But you don't have to make that journey alone. This book will be your powerful companion, a must-read guide that unlocks the secrets of your performance advantage and how you can achieve it. So I invite you to embrace your uniqueness, rise above the ordinary and become an extraordinary leader who leaves a lasting impact.

At this stage of your career, the 12 key PRINCIPLES and relevant observations shared in this book will give you what you need to know and what executive courses do not teach. I'm delighted to be sharing these invaluable insights with you, enabling you to save precious time and energy and bypass the trial and error that so often accompanies the journey to greatness. I want you to see this book as a comprehensive roadmap for the 12 PRINCIPLES that will drive profound transformation within you.

As an accomplished leader, you know that leadership is not just about achieving satisfactory results; it's about consistently driving extraordinary performance in yourself and others. Regardless of your professional field, the higher you go, the lonelier it becomes. So how do you keep ahead of the curve? How do you stay relevant and on top of your game? Retaining your high performance as a leader is no coincidence, nor is it down to talent or even luck.

Long-term success is rarely the result of one major breakthrough or accomplishment. It comes from consistently pursuing improvement in numerous small areas and making small yet pivotal changes when it really matters.

I've embarked on a quest to crack the code and identify the marginal, performance-critical shifts in thinking that power the competitive advantage in your leadership and career success. Focusing on these subtle but significant shifts will give you a distinct advantage that positions you ahead of the competition.

This book is for you if:

+ you're a successful, high-performing leader looking to take your leadership and career to the next level

+ you've reached a point in your career when the strategies you used to advance no longer serve you

+ you find it challenging to identify new growth opportunities or avenues for advancement, leading to a lack of motivation or a feeling of being stuck

+ you're a seasoned leader with several leadership programmes under your belt who's looking for a practical and impactful way to pivot your career

+ you're the successful leader who everyone describes as a high achiever but you're unsure what's next for you and how to get there.

THE PERFORMANCE ADVANTAGE encourages you to question the status quo, challenge the boundaries of your thinking and unlock the secrets to achieving exceptional performance across three key areas: your thinking, your leadership and your career success. This is not simply a collection of ideas or strategies; it's a call to action. It's also an invitation to step beyond your comfort zone and embrace the inherent challenges and opportunities that lie before you. As I share with you the principles, anecdotes and practical steps for driving pivotal shifts in your thinking, leadership and career while cultivating high performance, I want you to apply them boldly, knowing that true growth occurs only when knowledge is put into action.

Whether you're well advanced in your leadership journey with years of experience behind you or have just landed your first senior leadership role and are wondering what the next step of leadership development will entail, this book has been written for you. As opposed to accidental success based on the talent you may or may not be aware you possess, this stage of your leadership journey is about conscious, deliberate growth development. One of the best pieces of advice I've ever received was 'Understand what made you successful so you can recreate it'. I challenge you to do exactly this and follow in the footsteps of high-performing leaders with successful and fulfilling long-term careers who:

+ are focused on developing high-performance thinking, know their leadership superpower, are resilient and masters at subtracting complexity

+ understand the importance of their leadership, intentionally map their leadership journey, are advocates of self-care, embrace the concept of unlearning and have mastered the art of communication

+ are deliberate about their next career phase, have a clear personal brand, appreciate the power of influencing and embrace uncertainty through leading transformation and organisational change.

In writing this book I've given careful thought to the insights and information that will add the most value to you. I recognise the pressures and the time constraints that you face as a leader, so all the chapters can be read individually and are designed to encourage you to think differently. I don't want you to have a passive reading experience; I invite you to actively participate in your own transformation. Embrace the opportunity to reflect, grow and take ownership of your leadership journey.

Drawing on a wealth of personal experiences, I will share real life examples and practical insights that I hope will resonate with your own challenges and aspirations. To ensure your continued growth and progress, I've included a special self-development section with each principle, 'Reflect and Grow', with a series of thought-provoking coaching questions designed to ignite introspection and self-discovery. Paired with key takeaways, this section will empower you to internalise the knowledge gained and apply it directly to your leadership and career.

As you progress through *THE PERFORMANCE ADVANTAGE*, I encourage you to be honest and reflective about your leadership journey. It's perfectly normal not to have taken a deliberate approach before now, to have accepted positions or promotions because they were offered to you. But now is the time for you to take the driving seat and:

1. master habits and skills that will allow you to continue to be a high-performing leader
2. take your thinking, leadership and career to the next level
3. embrace confidence in yourself, your leadership and your career so that you can perform when it matters, which is a critical element of your continued success.

Now, let's embark on this transformative journey together. Prepare to be inspired, challenged and empowered as we navigate the terrain of leadership and career growth. The time has come to rethink, unlearn and rewrite your narrative while ascending to new levels of professional success.

PART 1

NEXT LEVEL SUCCESS

PRINCIPLE 1

DEVELOP HIGH-PERFORMANCE THINKING

We cannot change anything if we cannot change our thinking.
– Santosh Kalwar

High performance is not reserved for a select few. However, to be a high performer, you first need to think like one. It's a skill that can be mastered, and if you're serious about achieving your full potential it has to be your prime focus. High-performance thinking is about consistently achieving excellence.

In today's fast-paced and ever-evolving world, there's an unprecedented demand for exceptional performance. Your ability to consistently achieve outstanding results, inspire teams and navigate complex challenges is paramount. It's within this context that the significance of high-performance thinking comes to the fore.

Do we all share the same performance level? Absolutely not, and we don't need to. However, we do all possess the potential drive, determination and self-respect to be the very best version of ourselves. In that respect, everyone has the ability and the capacity to develop high-performance thinking skills. Doing so will not only impact your performance but will also significantly change the way that others relate to you and behave around you. By embracing high-performance thinking, you'll transcend your current capabilities, inspire greatness in others and create a culture of excellence that propels your team and organisation to unparalleled success.

I've always been described as a high achiever, which I accepted graciously but never truly identified with. But when I think about my journey I can understand where this came from. I made it from the back of that Grade 4 maths class in communist-ruled Hungary to funding my first business at 18 shortly after communism fell, selling it at 22 before venturing to London to ultimately become who I am today – an internationally recognised performance coach, trainer and speaker.

People were always interested in hearing my story, but my achievements often left me feeling somewhat cold and emotionless. It took a moment on a London stage, in front of a large audience, for me to understand who I really am. During that event, I experienced every speaker's worst nightmare. I was asked a question I wasn't sure how to answer; not because I didn't know the answer but because I realised that my thinking was very different to that of the person asking me the question. And that question was, 'Agnes, you are very successful. What would you do if it all suddenly disappeared tomorrow?'

I had to pause and think, because I'd never thought about it before. And then I wondered, why had I never thought about it? It's a pretty obvious question. I answered honestly, saying that if everything I'd achieved disappeared overnight, I had no fear of working. I told the audience that on the way to that event I'd seen an ad for shelf stackers in the window of a branch of Waitrose and I knew I'd be the best shelf stacker at any Waitrose store.

As I was walking offstage, I suddenly wondered where this confidence in my thinking had come from. Was it that I don't care what happens to my business or my career? Of course not; I care deeply. And then the realisation hit me: I don't care as much about the achievement as I do about the journey, the getting there, the process itself. The achievement is purely the output, and that's what gives me the confidence in my thinking that should things go wrong, I know I will be able to deal with it. I'm in control of my own thinking and won't be swayed by the fear of not achieving what I've set out to achieve.

Like me, you may have been described by others as a high achiever and have also struggled to identify with that description of yourself. Success is not about the achievement but about the process of achieving and being motivated by that process. Taking your leadership and career to the next level must be driven by performance versus just achievement. Try to visualise it as 'dancing with excellence'. I want you to list your key achievements and reflect on how you got there. What drove you? What excites you most about them? Most importantly, take time to really understand and appreciate the difference between performance and achievement.

Performance is the process of consistently performing at your best, focusing on continuous improvement and personal growth. Achievement refers to the specific goals or milestones you reach along the way. Achievements are important markers of success, but it's the commitment to high performance that drives long-term excellence and sustainable success.

I see performance as a mindset that transcends individual achievements. It's about consistently raising the bar, pushing your limits and striving for continual progress. By prioritising performance over achievement you'll be focused on the process rather than being solely fixated on the end result. This mindset fosters a sense of fulfilment and satisfaction in the journey itself. Keeping the emphasis on performance will also help you to maintain intrinsic motivation and a long-term perspective, even when you're faced with setbacks or temporary failures. It reinforces the idea that progress is more important than immediate outcomes.

While achievements may provide short-term satisfaction and recognition, it's high performance that leads you to sustained success and this will enable you, and ultimately your organisation, to continually raise standards and reach new levels of excellence. Leadership success is not solely defined by achievements or titles but also by the lasting impact and positive influence a leader has on their team and organisation. Prioritising performance and embracing marginal gains are essential in fostering effective leadership and driving long-term success. High performers think differently, but this makes them who they are regardless of what they do throughout their lives. They're driven by performance, not achievement, which allows them to achieve more as they automatically remove the biggest obstacle – fear.

High-performance thinking has to be your primary principle. It sets the stage for a transformative journey and establishes the importance of cultivating this mindset, not only for your personal growth but also to drive organisational success. By embracing high-performance thinking, you'll transcend your current capabilities, inspire greatness in others and create a culture of excellence that propels you and your organisation to unparalleled achievements.

Think like a high performer

In navigating the ever-shifting landscape of leadership, it becomes imperative to harness your cognitive capabilities to their fullest potential and think like a high performer. As a high-performance thinker, you don't sit back and wait for things to happen; you're proactive and take action. You see failure not as a bad thing but as an opportunity to learn and be successful. And you never place limits on your potential for growth and success. Becoming a high-performance thinker means stepping outside your comfort zone and it takes a conscious decision to master it.

Years of experience as an athlete and a coach taught Richard Young that medals aren't won on the day; they're the result of consistent principles and a personal performance system that has been followed for months and years. His book *Simplify* (2021) starts with 'your decision to be a high performer'. And in *Atomic Habits* (2018), writer and speaker James Clear states that 'we do not rise to the level of our goals; we fall to the level of our systems', where our systems include our habits, our thinking and the people we're connected to. If you want to change your habits and behaviours, you need to start with your thinking. And when you think like a high performer, you'll behave like a high performer.

As a high-performing leader, you create high-performance teams and lead high-performing organisations that deliver outstanding results and create impact. Your relentless pursuit of success demands a mastery of navigating your own thoughts, harnessing their power to unlock greatness. Make it your special ability to orchestrate excellence, because in the dynamic leadership landscape, your ability to channel your thoughts towards success is paramount.

High-performance thinking allows you to think more effectively and efficiently and is essential to maximising your performance as a leader. It's fundamental to achieving those crucial but subtle shifts to your leadership and career that will put you on track for success, and I will be sharing more of these with you in the coming PRINCIPLES.

The 'cognitive triangle' represents the interplay between our thoughts, emotions and behaviour. It's a powerful framework that can help you gain a deeper understanding of your own mental landscape and navigate it with precision. By recognising the influence of thoughts on emotions and behaviour, you can develop a heightened level of self-awareness and take deliberate actions to shape your outcomes.

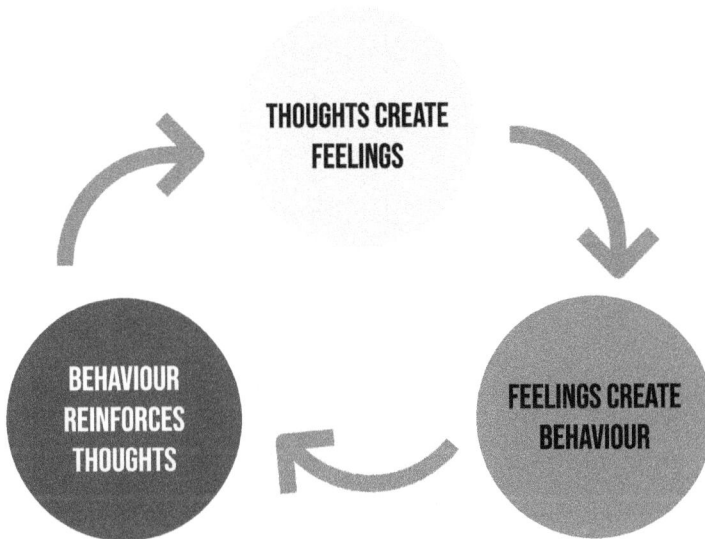

THOUGHTS CREATE FEELINGS

BEHAVIOUR REINFORCES THOUGHTS

FEELINGS CREATE BEHAVIOUR

Figure 1: The cognitive triangle

Thoughts are the internal dialogue, beliefs and interpretations we have about ourselves, others and the world around us. High-performing leaders cultivate positive and growth-oriented thoughts. They challenge negative or limiting beliefs, reframe setbacks as opportunities for growth and embrace a mindset of abundance and possibility.

Feelings are the responses triggered by our thoughts. They are the internal experiences that shape our mood, motivation and decision making. High-performing leaders understand the influence of emotions on their behaviour and performance. They develop emotional intelligence by recognising and managing their own emotions and empathising with the emotions of others. By harnessing your emotions effectively, you can inspire and motivate your teams, navigate challenges with resilience and build strong relationships.

Behaviour is the tangible expression of our thoughts and emotions. It includes our actions, communication style and leadership approach. As a high-performing leader, you align your behaviour with your goals, values and desired outcomes and demonstrate integrity, authenticity and accountability in your actions. Your positive thought patterns generate emotions that are conducive to high performance and inspiring your team to achieve remarkable results.

Becoming the leader you deserve to be begins with the way that you think, because your thoughts are the lenses through which you interpret the world around you. If you want to change your behaviour, change your thinking. This concept forms the basis of my PowerCoaching methodology and incorporated into all my training, presentations and speeches. Mastering the intricate relationship between thinking, emotions and behaviour is the key to unlocking your full potential as a high performer.

At some point, you may find yourself wondering how you'll notice a shift in your thinking. This pivotal moment is what I refer to as cognitive and emotional alignment – an experience where your thoughts, feelings and actions are in harmony. Suddenly, everything will click into place in a way that may not have been possible before.

Why is high-performance thinking so important?

I believe that high-performance thinking is the cornerstone on which exceptional outcomes are built. It's your catalyst for achieving and sustaining high performance. I constantly see how it navigates leaders to master those critical skills that will ultimately unlock their full potential, driving them towards extraordinary levels of achievement.

High-performance thinking enables you to make informed decisions, solve complex problems and lead your organisation to success. As a high-performance leader, you're able to adapt your style of leadership to any situation at any given time, which in the current climate of change and uncertainty is absolutely vital. You'll have achieved mastery of your thinking, emotions and behaviours and as a result will get the best out of yourself and your team in the most exceptional of circumstances. And when your team share high-performance thinking skills, they'll be better equipped to make effective decisions, solve problems and navigate challenges.

High performance in action

High-performance thinkers are defined by several abilities, traits and characteristics, some more critical to high-performance leadership than others. But what does high-performance thinking look like in action?

A few years ago, a large global manufacturer based in South America was looking for a new CEO to turn the company around. It had faced numerous challenges, including intense competition, rising costs and a decline in customer satisfaction. Something needed to change and quickly and there was no better person for the job than my former client Sarah, a seasoned executive renowned for her high-performance thinking and her track record of turning struggling organisations into powerhouses of success. She understood that transformation would come through harnessing the power of prioritisation, cognitive load management and effective decision making.

Sarah wasted no time in implementing her vision for the company. She gathered her team and shared her unwavering commitment to high performance. Together, they embarked on a journey of transformation. With a keen eye for discerning what truly mattered and focusing on marginal gains, Sarah guided her team in identifying the critical objectives that would drive the most significant results. By focusing their efforts on these strategic priorities, they could channel their energy and resources towards meaningful outcomes.

Sarah then introduced the concept of cognitive load management. She understood that overwhelmed minds lead to below-par performance. She encouraged her team to streamline processes, eliminate unnecessary complexities and provide clear guidance and support. By reducing cognitive load, team members could direct their attention and energy towards critical tasks, ensuring optimal performance and avoiding burnout.

Effective decision making was another cornerstone of Sarah's leadership philosophy. She instilled a culture of evidence-based decision making, where data and insights took precedence over subjective opinions. Sarah empowered her team to leverage analytics, market research and customer feedback to inform their choices. This approach not only increased the accuracy of decision making but also fostered a sense of ownership and accountability among team members.

As the months passed, the impact of Sarah's high-performance thinking became evident. The organisation experienced a significant turnaround. Under Sarah's leadership, it rose to new heights. Market share expanded, profitability soared and employee morale reached unprecedented levels. The transformation was nothing short of remarkable and it was a testament to the power of high-performance thinking in driving exceptional results.

At this stage of your career, small shifts towards developing your thinking will have a positive impact on all the attributes that are critical elements of your leadership success.

I invite you to reflect on Sarah's story and think about how you can apply these principles in your own leadership journey. Embrace the transformative potential of high-performance thinking and unlock the path to unparalleled success. The time for you to make your mark is now.

Observations

As a seasoned leadership coach I've had the privilege of engaging in conversations and working with countless high-performing leaders. Through these interactions, I've gleaned the pivotal insight of how the power of marginal gains consistently emerges as the bedrock of their continued success.

High-performance thinking is critical to achieving marginal gains and understanding marginal gains is crucial to becoming a high-performance thinker. So you must be able to analyse your performance and identify areas for improvement, be willing to experiment with new approaches, seek out feedback and be open to learning and adapting.

To achieve marginal gains, you must set specific, measurable goals and identify the small improvements that can be made in various areas to achieve those goals. The marginal gains theory (that improving and optimising your performance by a small amount across a number of different areas will lead to much more significant, noticeable improvements overall) has been widely used in sports for many years.

In his book *Black Box Thinking* (2016) Matthew Syed shares how 'Marginal gains is not about making small changes and hoping they fly. Rather, it is about breaking down a big problem into small parts in order to rigorously establish what works and what doesn't.'

Arguably the best example of high-performance thinking through marginal gains is that of Dave Brailsford, former coach of the British cycling team. In 2003, Brailsford took over the British cycling team, which had never won a gold medal at the Olympics. His goal was to turn the team into a world-class organisation and win the Tour de France, which no British rider had ever done. To achieve this,

Brailsford employed a philosophy of marginal gains. He believed that by making small improvements in every aspect of the team's performance, he could create a significant overall improvement.

Brailsford and his team analysed every aspect of the team's performance, from the riders' training regimens to the design of their bikes. They looked for ways to make small, incremental improvements in each area – for example, optimising the riders' diets to ensure they were getting the right nutrients and fuel for their bodies. They also improved the design of the bikes to reduce wind resistance and increase speed.

Over time, these small improvements led to significant improvements in the British cycling team's performance. In 2008, they won eight gold medals at the Beijing Olympics and in 2012, they won the Tour de France. Brailsford's approach to high-performance thinking through marginal gains demonstrates the power of making small improvements in every aspect of your performance, especially when you're already a high performer or a leader with many years of experience. I had the enormous privilege of observing the power of marginal gains in action from my back garden during the 2012 London Olympics, when I watched Bradley Wiggins of the British cycling team ride to success as he negotiated the roundabout at high speed on Seven Hills Road in Weybridge. As a performance coach myself, it was a moment to cherish.

When you adopt a high-performance mindset, you set yourself up for success. More importantly, you're more likely to engage in high-performance behaviours that drive you towards your goals. In this way, as a high-performance thinker you become a high-performance leader who goes on to lead high-performing teams in high-performing organisations. The result is the creation of an organisational culture where there are no limitations on growth and development. This doesn't mean that everyone is expected to achieve the same level of performance or share the same performance targets. What it does mean is that everybody is performing at their highest level in terms of their own potential, ability and skills. Growth is open ended. There are no limits.

Developing high-performance thinking takes time, effort and persistence. Here are my top three observations of leaders who are masters of high-performance thinking.

Observation #1: They are their own performance leader and have made a conscious decision to be a high performer

Becoming a high-performance leader is a conscious decision. It's about taking ownership of your own performance, setting high standards for yourself and committing to continuous improvement in every aspect of your work. It's also about focusing your energy and attention on the tasks that matter most and constantly seeking out new opportunities to learn and grow.

As a high performer you thrive on expanding your comfort zone and fearlessly embrace ambiguity. You understand that true growth lies just beyond the boundaries of familiarity and by willingly stepping into the unknown, you open yourself up to new perspectives, fresh challenges and opportunities for advancement. While this may create a sense of fear or trepidation in some individuals, high-performing leaders and thinkers find this challenge exciting and intrinsically motivating, and this is infectious.

As individuals we all have our comfort zone and outside that lies the fear zone. Beyond that is the learning and development zone. What might appear daunting for one person is exciting to another. One important characteristic that I'm constantly aware of when working with high-performance thinkers is their eagerness to embrace uncertainty and move towards challenges, even when they don't know what the outcome will be. It's a characteristic that many acquire as they develop their high-performance thinking. Letting go of fear is key. Moreover, high-performance leaders create cultures and environments where people can think beyond and also act beyond what they previously thought was the limit of their potential.

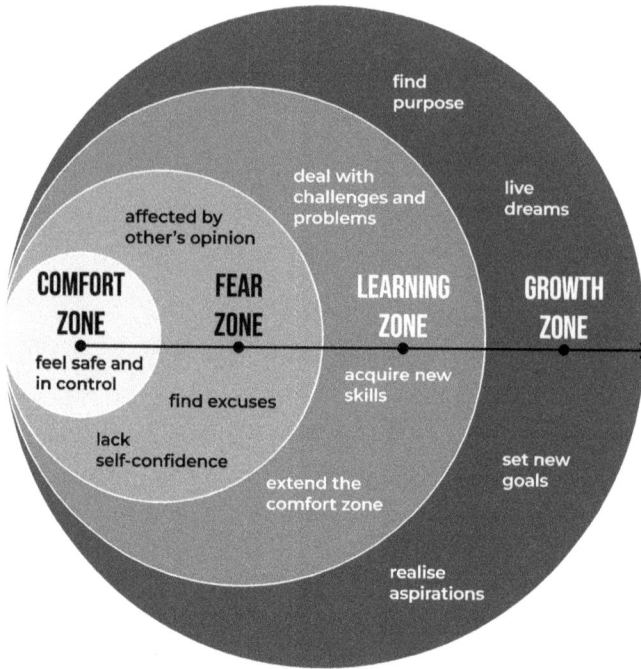

Figure 2: Beyond the comfort zone

What kind of leader do you choose to be? It's a question that I frequently put to the leaders I have the privilege to meet on their journeys. Leadership is a choice and a decision, not a position. It's a conscious decision to unlock your potential and ultimately that of others.

High-performing leaders have a clear purpose that keeps them focused and motivated. Knowing who you are and what you stand for are important factors in determining the type of leader you're destined to be. Being consistent comes from knowing what your values are so that in high-pressure situations your decisions are consistent. Empathy, self-awareness and resilience are critical, as is having the trust of the people around you.

Regardless of your current role or title, your journey to becoming a high-performance leader begins when you empower yourself to be the leader you deserve to be and surround yourself with others who share the same high-performance mindset. The decision to be a high performer starts with your thinking and your commitment to yourself. As the former NFL coach Tom Flores once said, 'Total commitment is paramount to reaching the ultimate performance,' and that is a principle with which I wholeheartedly agree.

Every day you have the opportunity to make a choice about how you'll lead yourself and those around you. Becoming a high-performance leader requires you to make a conscious decision to be one. This means committing to developing the skills, mindset and habits that you need to achieve exceptional results. It means setting high standards for yourself and never settling for mediocrity. It means being willing to take risks, make mistakes and learn from your failures. And it means being committed to continuous improvement, always striving to be better today than you were yesterday. Invest in your personal and professional development by seeking out learning opportunities that will help you build the skills and knowledge you need to excel in your role. This can include attending workshops, reading books or articles and seeking out mentorship or coaching.

Jeff Bezos, founder and former CEO of Amazon, made a conscious decision to become a high-performance leader. Known for his relentless focus on achieving exceptional results, he consciously made the decision early on in his career to set high standards for himself and his team. He also invested heavily in his own personal and professional development, reading voraciously, attending conferences and workshops and seeking out mentorship and advice from other successful leaders. He was committed to lifelong learning and never stopped finding ways to improve himself. Bezos was also known for his strong work ethic. He was willing to put in long hours and push himself and his team to achieve more. He had a deep sense of purpose and was always driven to make a difference in the world. He recognised the importance of building strong relationships with his team members and stakeholders and was known for his direct communication style and willingness to listen to feedback and ideas from others. The culture he built at Amazon was founded on innovation, risk-taking and customer obsession and he inspired his team to think big and achieve their best.

I challenge you to learn from his example and many other leaders who consciously choose to be their own performance leader and take high-performance thinking seriously.

Observation #2: They see thinking as a discipline and are designers of the architecture of their own thinking

Great power comes from knowing what you don't know. It inspires you to have an open mind and a thirst for learning. When you acquire practical knowledge it gives you an advantage. It's fundamental for any high-performing leader to appreciate the power of continual learning and that consistent, small shifts will make all the difference.

You can't bring about change unless you view thinking as a discipline. It requires a committed desire to learn more and be a better version of yourself, both personally and professionally. Discipline needs to be continual, consistent and conscious. Designing the architecture of your thinking with regular habits allows you to grow and enable others around you to take their thinking to another level. Thinking is skilled work.

Thinking about high-performance thinking can sound like an abstract concept but it's one that's extremely effective. Thinking requires time and space and this is exactly what high performers do regularly, allocating thinking blocks in their diary, engaging with their leadership inner circle for collaborative thinking and experimenting with different thinking strategies.

Take the example of Howard Schultz, the former CEO of Starbucks. Schultz understood the importance of reflection and analysis in driving the success of his company. He made it a habit to set aside time each day to reflect on Starbucks' mission, values and strategic goals. By investing time and energy into thinking deeply about his company's direction, Schultz was able to make better decisions and lead his team more effectively.

One of the keys to high-performance thinking is making a deliberate effort to think critically and strategically. This requires discipline, focus and a willingness to challenge assumptions and consider alternative perspectives.

Leaders need to develop the habit of asking powerful questions to inspire their team and drive innovation. Jeff Weiner, the former CEO of LinkedIn, was a master at asking thought-provoking questions that challenged his team members to think deeply and creatively. By encouraging his team to think beyond the status quo and explore new possibilities, Weiner was able to drive innovation and growth within his company.

High-performance thinking is a combination of mindset, habits and skills that will enable you to operate at your best and bring out the best in your team. When you think critically and strategically you're more likely to make sound decisions and achieve exceptional results. Be your own high-performance architect and do not underestimate the power of discipline for your thinking.

Observation #3: They understand that high performance is not a solo journey and always keep others in mind

High-performance leaders are constantly asking themselves what success looks like for their team and others around them, including those in their leadership inner circle. But more important questions to ask yourself are: who's in your leadership inner circle, who should be in it and why does it matter?

If you want to create a greater impact, you need to empower and connect with others who are part of your high-performance journey from the outset. This is where you start to build your inner circle, a group of people who are high performers themselves, who will challenge you, not obstructively but objectively, taking on the role of devil's advocates. This is so important because without having people who will challenge you, you'll be surrounded by people who agree with you, which will do nothing for the development and growth of your high-performance thinking and leadership skills. A broad perspective is crucial to challenging your thinking and taking it to a new level of performance.

In my experience, the one thing that leaders don't do enough of is ask questions in order to adopt the type of big-picture thinking that's essential for maximising performance. Leadership isn't about knowing all the answers, nor is it about everybody coming to you with problems that you'll provide solutions to. While there's a time and place for that, the most important aspect of leadership is encouraging others to grow and develop and to ask the right questions. How many questions have you asked this week?

Bill Gates, the co-founder of Microsoft, is widely regarded as one of the most successful and innovative leaders of our time but he recognises that his success is due in large part to the contributions of his team members. In fact, Gates has said that his ability to attract and retain talented people has been one of the key factors in his success.

It's easy to fall into the trap of thinking that high-performance leadership is a solo journey. After all, leaders are often held up as the face of success and achievement within their organisations. In truth, it's not a solo journey for any leader. One of the most important things you can do to achieve high performance is to build strong relationships and foster a culture of collaboration within your organisation. By working together and leveraging the strengths and expertise of their team members, you'll achieve more than you ever could on your own.

REFLECT AND GROW

Here are the top three key takeaways from PRINCIPLE 1:

+ *If you want to be a high performer, you need to think like one: your thinking will drive your feelings and ultimately your behaviour.*

+ *Know the difference between performance and achievement – it will make the biggest difference in your perspective and long-term leadership and career success.*

+ *Embrace the power of marginal gains. Be your own performance manager, turn your thinking into a discipline and appreciate that high performance is not a solo journey.*

Reflect on the three points below:

+ *What does high performance mean to you at this stage of your career?*

+ *How will you incorporate high-performance thinking into your own, your team's and your organisation's leadership practice?*

+ *Identify one area of focus for the next six months that will best allow you to take your performance and your team's performance to the next level. This will be your and your team's high-performance thinking goal.*

YOUR PERFORMANCE ADVANTAGE HACK

Allocate time in your diary to review and reflect on high performance. It can be ten minutes a week to ten minutes a day. This discipline will make a huge difference to your development as a high-performance thinker.

PRINCIPLE (2)

DISCOVER YOUR LEADERSHIP SUPERPOWER

Mastering others is strength; mastering yourself is a true power. – Lao Tzu

What is your leadership superpower? Do you know the superpowers of others around you? Right now you're probably wondering what constitutes a leadership superpower and why it matters. To explain, when I talk about superpowers, I'm not talking about the list of strengths that you know you possess and are rigorously tested during interviews and assessments. Your superpower is the distinct skill or attribute that sets you apart from other leaders and makes you especially impactful in your role. It's your most potent leadership asset.

So what's your superpower? I've never met a leader who didn't have one but I've met plenty who were unaware of it. Your initial reaction may be to see this as boasting. However, identifying your superpower is about growing your leadership confidence. We all have superpowers but aren't always fully aware of what they are or how they positively affect those around us. You may be hesitant about naming them yourself but you can't lead at your best without knowing who you are at your best.

At the age of 22, just after I'd sold my first business, I was on a mission to find out what had made me successful so that I could recreate it. This was when I discovered my superpower: resilience. I'll be honest – at that stage I didn't know that was what it was called. But in reflecting on my past, I knew I had an inner strength, a quality that had helped me endure a childhood lacking in nurture and navigate years of education in the communist system while seeking mental escape from reality. It drove me across endless bridges and huge challenges, including that of dealing with success as a young female entrepreneur. In the first four years of running my business, there was one common denominator, which was obvious to others but less so to me: my ability to move forward and make decisions when it mattered. Resilience was and still is my superpower.

It kept me ahead of the game and gave me the confidence to push forward in the most extraordinary of circumstances when invariably I was the youngest in the room. As one of my colleagues in the speaking profession would say, 'Agnes, you're slowly growing into your wisdom.' While I bravely heeded my grandfather's advice in the back of that maths class, it hasn't been an easy journey and I've often tapped into my superpower along the way.

Your leadership superpower is not necessarily something that no one else has but it will elevate all your other strengths and enable your high performance. And it may not be what you think. A conversation with one of my CFO clients in Dubai on this topic recently demonstrated this. She was confident that her incredible analytical skill was her superpower and went into extreme detail to prove her point. So I asked her what differentiated her from her peers who are equally analytical and what enabled her to lead a successful and high-performing team of 900. How did others describe her? She alluded to the fact that her ability to build and maintain strong relationships was frequently recognised. A leader with this superpower has the emotional intelligence to connect with her team members on a personal level, build trust and create a sense of psychological safety. This enables her to create an environment where team members feel comfortable sharing their ideas, taking risks and making mistakes, knowing they have support from her and the team.

Like every other developed leader I've ever met, you'll have at least one superpower and leveraging that is the most effective way of influencing your teams and achieving the results that you want. It's the common denominator of your success that ensures that you continue to excel, even during times of uncertainty, crisis and transformation. It's the one single driving factor that you can always rely on and it gives you that all-important competitive advantage for your leadership and career success.

It may feel strange to be thinking about your superpower – indeed, you may never have considered it before – but it will prove to be a valuable asset on your leadership journey, helping you overcome the challenges you'll face along the way. In many ways, your superpower is your engine and the more you understand it, the more powerful it will become.

Cultivating your superpower

Leadership isn't about creating a strategy on your own and then telling others what to do, nor is it about having all the answers. It's about having an awareness of your strengths and development areas as well as an understanding of the people you work with, so you can support them with their wellbeing, personal growth and performance.

Identifying and cultivating your superpower is one of the keys to becoming an effective, high-performing leader. It could be exceptional communication skills, a talent for strategic thinking or the ability to connect with people on a personal level. It could be positivity, vision or empathy. Whatever it is, your superpower will be unique to you and it will truly drive your success.

In *StrengthsFinder 2.0* (2007), author and researcher Tom Rath states, 'You cannot be anything you want to be – but you can be a whole lot more of who you already are.' This is a powerful statement that should make you stop comparing yourself to others and start focusing more of your time and attention on your own leadership and performance.

Two of the first questions I ask leaders are:

+ What is your leadership superpower?
+ Do you know how to find it?

It's important to identify your leadership superpower because it will help you leverage your strengths and lead more effectively. By understanding what sets you apart as a leader, you can utilise your skills more effectively in driving your team to success. In addition, identifying your superpower enables you to delegate responsibilities that don't align with your strengths, which will increase team efficiency and productivity.

You and I know that few challenges loom as large as changing the culture of an organisation. Now, imagine the scale of that challenge magnified when the organisation in question boasts a staggering 114,000 employees spread across the globe and generates a remarkable $86 billion in revenue. Cast your mind back to 2014, a pivotal year that marked the commencement of Satya Nadella's tenure as CEO of Microsoft. The technology giant, already deeply entrenched in the fabric of the industry, was poised for a new era of growth and reinvention under his guidance. However, a fundamental shift was required, one that extended beyond mere strategic adjustments or operational efficiencies. Nadella recognised that to truly propel Microsoft into the future, a cultural transformation was essential.

The task before Nadella was akin to steering a mammoth ship in a new direction. The existing culture within Microsoft had its merits but it also carried ingrained behaviours, processes and mindsets that required a recalibration to meet the demands of a rapidly evolving digital landscape. Nadella understood that transforming such a colossal organisation necessitated a delicate balance of conviction, vision and strategic action but most importantly he needed to tap into his ability to create a culture that valued empathy and collaboration, which he believed was business critical in order to foster innovation and creativity.

Nadella implemented a number of changes to create this culture, including redefining Microsoft's mission statement to focus on empowering people and organisations rather than just selling products. Even if it meant making mistakes, he also encouraged employees to experiment and take risks and emphasised the importance of learning from failure.

These changes paid off as, according to the BBC, Microsoft's stock price more than tripled during Nadella's tenure as CEO and the company became known for its innovation and collaboration (Kelly 2019). Nadella's superpower of creating a culture of empathy and collaboration was instrumental in this success, as it allowed Microsoft to attract and retain top talent, foster a sense of belonging and purpose among employees and create a more positive and productive work environment.

The results of Nadella's cultural transformation have been nothing short of extraordinary. Under his stewardship, Microsoft's revenue has nearly doubled, demonstrating the tangible impact of a revitalised culture on organisational performance. The company has re-established itself as a trailblazer in the technology industry, leading the charge in areas such as cloud computing, artificial intelligence and digital transformation.

Why is it important to find your leadership superpower?

I'm all about maximising the time I spend on things that truly make a difference and I'm sure you feel the same. Uncovering your superpower is a game changer for your leadership journey and will be one of the best investments you can make for the following reasons:

+ It boosts your confidence and enhances your sense of purpose and self-belief, all of which will allow you to lead more effectively. When you're confident in your abilities, others will feel confident in following your lead.

+ It allows you to focus your efforts. By identifying your superpower, you can focus your energy and resources on the areas where you're the most effective. You can achieve more in less time and you're less likely to waste time and resources on activities that don't play to your strengths.

+ It helps you to build a strong team. A good leader knows that they can't do everything alone. By identifying your superpower, you can bring in team members who complement your skills and help you achieve your goals more quickly and effectively.

+ It sets you apart from the competition. In today's crowded marketplace, it's more important than ever to be a leader who stands out. By identifying and developing your superpower, you can differentiate yourself from other leaders and build a unique personal leadership brand that others will remember. It's also crucial to building your resilience, as you'll discover in the next chapter.

How do you find your superpower?

During my coaching and training sessions, I often do an exercise where I ask someone to identify their leadership superpower. Most people will name one of their strengths. Some people will say they don't know, and I'm delighted when that happens. People need to recognise that they don't have all the answers all the time and that they don't fully know themselves.

You may be somebody who has always been described as a good communicator. But is that your superpower? Or is it some element of communication that makes you exceptional? Your leadership superpower could be listening, active listening, connected listening or visualisation. It could be observation skills, empathy or curiosity.

As you know, my superpower is resilience. But if you were to ask other people what my superpower is they would probably say it's my passion, because I'm extremely passionate about everything; or perhaps curiosity. I'm endlessly curious but resilience drives my passion and curiosity. What enables me to leverage all my strengths, embrace challenge and uncertainty yet remain passionate and curious is my superpower: resilience.

Finding your superpower begins with a reflective process; without it, you can't analyse your behaviour. You need to reflect to understand yourself. Reflection is not judgement but reserving judgement and minimising bias. Reflect on your past successes. Think back to times and events when you were particularly effective as a leader. What skills or attributes did you use to achieve those successes? This could provide you with a clue as to what your superpower might be.

Ask for feedback from colleagues, employees and others on what they see as your strengths as a leader. Other people are often able to see things about us that we don't see ourselves. But don't just ask for feedback; take it. More than that, use it to make meaningful changes. Taking feedback requires humility, self-awareness and a willingness to learn and grow as a leader. And don't just ask for feedback from people you think are good at giving feedback or those you think know you well or will tell you what you want to hear. Seek feedback from a broad range of individuals. You'll be surprised how consistent it can be. Often the biggest 'aha' moment occurs when that consistent feedback comes from the person or the place that you were least expecting it from. Don't limit yourself when you're identifying your superpower.

Try new things. Don't be afraid to experiment with new leadership approaches and techniques. You might discover a new skill or talent that you didn't know you had.

I started drumming at the age of 40. Drums are not the easiest instruments to play, and I'm not the best drummer in the world nor planning to be a professional musician. What drove me to start drumming and what has allowed me to make good progress is not my physical strength or ability to read music – it's my relentless resilience.

Practise, practise, practise. Once you've identified your superpower you must consciously cultivate and refine it. Like any skill, it takes practice to become truly great at something. While practising will reinforce your superpower, it's also a tracking mechanism, a way of confirming that this skill or trait is your superpower.

Practising your leadership superpower involves consistent and deliberate action, which can help you develop habits that support your leadership growth and development. When you practise your superpower on a regular basis, you're essentially training your brain to automatically respond in a certain way when faced with similar situations. For example, if your superpower is your ability to remain calm and composed under pressure, you can practise mindfulness and stress-reducing techniques such as meditation, deep breathing or visualisation. Over time, these practices will become habitual, allowing you to respond in a calm and collected manner when faced with challenging situations.

Similarly, if your superpower is your ability to build strong relationships, you should practise active listening, empathy and effective communication skills. By consistently using these skills, you'll develop a habit of building positive relationships with others, which strengthens your leadership impact.

Developing habits that support your leadership superpower is important because it can lead to more consistent and effective leadership behaviours. By making these behaviours automatic, you can conserve cognitive resources and reduce decision fatigue, allowing you to focus on other areas of leadership development.

Knowing your superpower is important, but avoid becoming obsessed and fixated on finding it immediately. It may happen when you get to the end of this book, or it may not happen until several months later when you reflect. However, unless you start your journey of discovery, your superpower will remain elusive.

Finding and taking ownership of your leadership superpower is essential to winning the trust and confidence of those around you and making a lasting impact. By focusing on your strengths and developing your unique abilities, you can build a strong team, stand out from the competition and lead confidently and purposefully. So take the time to reflect on your strengths, experiment with new approaches and cultivate your superpower. The results will be worth the effort.

Observations

I want you to imagine that your leadership superpower is a special ingredient – a spice or a secret sauce that turns your dish into something extra special. We can all recall those moments during a dinner party when someone asks 'What's in this dish? Can I have the recipe?' You may have identified many strengths throughout your career through feedback and performance reviews but can you answer this question: what is it that truly differentiates you from other leaders with similar strengths?

This is your leadership superpower. It's your fingerprint, your leadership identity and it gives you an edge – a subtle edge, especially when the going gets tough. It's something that you can tap into during situations that take you outside your comfort zone, especially in times of difficulty and challenge when your leadership is being tested to the full.

These are my top three observations on how leaders use their superpowers to increase their performance, leadership impact and success.

Observation #1: They are highly observant and regularly reflect on their performance and success, as well as their mistakes

As a leader you should reflect regularly on how your superpower contributes to your success. However, the real magic happens when you continually strive to improve in the process, identifying areas for growth and development, recognising your strengths and leveraging them to achieve your goals.

Reflecting on your mistakes and failures and learning from them will reap additional benefits. Research published by *Personnel Psychology* has shown that when leaders take time to reflect on what they learned from their errors, they show more humility – a quality that makes them more effective (Hu et al 2022).

Discussing these observations with trusted colleagues will provide you with valuable insights and feedback, as well as support and encouragement. It's an effective way to gain new perspectives, insights and ideas while also identifying gaps in understanding or areas where you may need some additional support.

By regularly reflecting on your performance you'll find it easier to identify the subtle shifts and make the micro observations that create a detailed pattern of information about your leadership performance and progress. Reflecting on your performance involves taking a step back from day-to-day activities to analyse your actions and decisions. It's an opportunity to learn from successes and failures and make the necessary adjustments to improve your future performance. It requires a willingness to take risks, try new approaches and learn from mistakes. Highly observant leaders who embrace this mindset are far better able to adapt to changing circumstances and achieve their goals.

One example of a leader who identified and utilised her superpower is Angela Merkel, the former chancellor of Germany. Merkel's superpower was her ability to build strong relationships with other world leaders and navigate complex diplomatic negotiations. She had a deep understanding of the political landscape and was able to use her emotional intelligence to establish trust and rapport with her counterparts. This allowed her to successfully negotiate numerous agreements, including the European Union's bailout of Greece in 2010.

Merkel's ability to build strong relationships was crucial in the face of several global crises, including the Syrian refugee crisis and the Brexit vote. Her leadership during these crises demonstrated her superpower in action, as she was able to work with other world leaders to find solutions and maintain stability. Merkel's superpower also allowed her to successfully manage the diverse interests and personalities within her own political party and coalition government.

Merkel's success as a leader is a testament to the importance of identifying and utilising your superpower in leadership through regular reflections. By leveraging her unique strengths, Merkel was able to build strong relationships, navigate complex negotiations and lead her country through challenging times.

Observation #2: They know how to unlock their leadership superpower and have developed strategies for doing so when it matters

Knowing what your leadership superpower is and how it can enhance your performance is a strong position to be in. However, waiting for it to occur naturally won't lead to consistent leadership success. You need to develop specific strategies for tapping into your superpower when you need it the most – for example, when dealing with crises or facing challenging situations.

The strategy that I use to unlock my superpower is best described as tapping into my flow state – that sense of ease you experience when things fall into place and the feeling of energised focus that you get when you're completely immersed in a particular activity. In order to harness this as a strategy for quickly unlocking and activating your superpower you must create a mental and physical environment that facilitates that flow state.

It's important to develop an infallible strategy or critical pathway that will unlock your leadership superpower. Awareness of your superpower is not enough. If you're going to maximise your success and performance, you need to make it a reality. Try thinking of a time or an occasion when you were successful in rapidly unlocking your leadership superpower. Think about how that happened, how you were thinking and feeling in the moment and what you need to do to recreate it.

I've had to call on my superpower many times during my career, for example, when I was overcoming the huge challenges of setting up my first business as a young female entrepreneur, selling that business and heading for the UK and London, a city and a country so very different from my native Hungary. I spent 20 years there before moving to Germany, another new country with a new culture and new challenges. At the age of 50, I wrote my first book, which demanded focus, discipline and commitment on a completely different level. My resilience has helped me to overcome all these challenges. It allows me to perform at a consistently high level. For example, I might have to deliver six coaching sessions in one day – a day that can also be full of distractions and interruptions. However, my resilience ensures the last session is delivered as consistently as the first. To maintain high performance I tap into my superpower, engage it and activate it. I will focus on the subject of resilience and how to build it (not necessarily as your superpower) in PRINCIPLE 3.

Observation #3: They systematically develop their leadership superpower

I make no secret of the fact that I'm not a fan of developing weaknesses. This may surprise you, coming from a trainer and coach – but stay with me on this. Logic dictates that your weaknesses represent your greatest development opportunities. People have long focused on addressing their weaknesses in order to increase their chances of success. However, recent thinking suggests that this approach may not be the most effective and certainly not the best way of honing essential leadership skills. It argues that when leaders, teams, cultures and individuals focus on their strengths, they have a better chance of succeeding than if they focus on improving deficiencies. Motivational speaker and management consultant Marcus Buckingham (2019) said, 'If you want to grow, you need to focus on skills and practices that are already strong. Those strengths, rather than your weaknesses, should guide your improvement.'

You need to identify your superpower, cultivate it and systematically develop it. This is the behaviour I see in high-performing leaders all the time. Leaders who use their leadership superpower well are acutely aware that nothing lasts forever. For example, I've heard so many times people describing themselves as 'an effective communicator'. There's nothing wrong with that, but are you still as effective as you used to be? Is it still your secret ingredient? Is it really your superpower?

To make it a superpower, make it *your* superpower. Finding out what yours is involves others. It's not an instant process but it will lead to a much more successful leadership journey. But you need to use it or lose it and you need to keep developing it. It's no different from the way that top athletes work on their fitness or physique, exercising relentlessly and practising constantly to stay at the top of their game.

Unless you dedicate time and effort to developing your superpower, it won't be your lasting competitive advantage. Others won't stop developing theirs. Climbing the career ladder and taking up different roles with increased responsibilities will require you to take your leadership superpower to the next level. But you'll end up with a false self-perception if, in reality, it's no longer your competitive advantage. You'll find yourself in situations where your superpower is the key to success, only to end up frustrated because it's no longer your superpower.

The higher you go, the thinner the air becomes and as a leader you need that competitive advantage of knowing which unique asset you're bringing to the table in an environment where everybody is a good communicator or everybody can make good decisions in difficult times. Keep your leadership superpower relevant, develop it continuously and stay connected to those in your leadership inner circle who inspire and challenge you.

REFLECT AND GROW

Here are the top three key takeaways from PRINCIPLE 2:

+ *Your leadership superpower is your most valuable asset – spend time and energy discovering and embracing it. It will be your biggest competitive advantage.*

+ *Invest effort in consciously developing your leadership superpower – if you don't, it won't be your competitive advantage forever.*

+ *Embrace the power of observation. This is the most important action you can take to understand your own and others' leadership superpowers, because it's the 'special spice' that will elevate your strength and that of others.*

Reflect on the three points below:

+ *Reflect on your past successes. Think about times in your life when you've achieved success as a leader, whether in your personal or professional life. What strengths did you draw upon to achieve these successes? Were there any particular skills or abilities that were critical to your success?*

+ *Ask for feedback from colleagues, friends or family members who know you well and have observed you in a leadership role. What do they see as your strengths as a leader? Are there any particular skills or abilities that you seem to excel at?*

+ *Take a personality or leadership assessment. There are many assessments available that can help you identify your strengths and weaknesses as a leader. For example, DISC personality profiling (See PRINCIPLE 7) can help you understand your personality type and how it relates to your leadership style. This will enable you to understand how others perceive you and to embrace your leadership superpower more impactfully.*

YOUR PERFORMANCE ADVANTAGE HACK

Use the concept of leadership superpowers in your selection and recruitment process. It will encourage applicants to approach the typical strength-related questions differently. Ask about their leadership superpower during the interview.

PRINCIPLE 3

EMBRACE THE POWER OF RESILIENCE

Resilience is often endurance with direction. – Eric Greitens

For high performers, mental resilience is a powerful source of competitive advantage. It's not about being tough and emotionless but about your capacity to quickly turn things around and recover confidently, moving forward as fast as possible. Being resilient might be tough but it's not about being tough.

Let me take you back to 4 April 1996 and one of the best opportunities I've had to observe resilience on live TV. I'm not a golfing fan and certainly not an expert on the sport but on that day I couldn't stop watching Nick Faldo's victory at the US Masters, which was a testament to his resilience on so many levels. On entering the tournament, Faldo wasn't in top form. A win had eluded him for two years. But on the last day, he was playing against the tournament leader Greg Norman. He started slowly and at one point was six shots behind Norman, who looked set for a straightforward win. Faldo started that day knowing there were 18 holes and 18 opportunities ahead. Through consistency and resilience, he took the lead at the 16th, only to hit his tee shot into the woods. Instead of panicking, he remained calm and focused and tapped into his resilience, which allowed him to optimise his performance. When Norman hit a ball into the water he was unable to tap into his resilience. This was the turning point that significantly contributed to Faldo's victory.

Why am I telling you this? First, from a personal point of view, this was the moment when I consciously began focusing on and developing my resilience, instead of politely agreeing with everyone who had been telling me since my childhood how resilient I was. The second and most important reason is that one of the questions I'm asked most frequently is this: if I could develop just one skill for leaders, what would it be? Without hesitation, I say resilience. Therefore I can't possibly be your companion on your leadership journey without teaching you how to tap into and develop your resilience.

What does resilience mean to you? The topic is often discussed but much misunderstood. I recall talking to a senior leader from a financial organisation, someone who could be described as being on top of his career. Before we started our coaching programme he wanted to share with me something that was important to him and it was something I hear quite often. He said, 'Agnes, you know what, I'm not actually very resilient.' I asked, 'How do you know?' His response was, 'Because I'm not tough.'

Let me make a clear statement before you read any further. As I said at the start of this chapter, resilience is not about being tough. It's about how quickly you can deal with, navigate and move forward after an event or situation, expected or unexpected, that presents you with challenges. And I'm going to show you how, as a high-performing leader, you can build your resilience.

What is resilience?

According to the American Psychological Association's *Dictionary of Psychology*, resilience is 'the process and outcome of successfully adapting to difficult or challenging life experiences, especially through mental, emotional and behavioural flexibility and adjustment to external and internal demands'.

I view resilience as the ability to return to your optimum performance after an occurrence that challenges you emotionally, psychologically or socially. Developing resilience can help you cope adaptively and bounce back after changes, challenges, setbacks, disappointments and failures. However, it's equally important in the context of success. People demonstrate resilience far more often than they think – and that includes you. Yet resilience remains both intriguing and hard to define. Why does one person embrace challenge and difficulty while another crumbles? It's not all about experiencing hard times.

To fully appreciate the power of resilience and the impact it can have on your leadership and performance at individual, team or organisational level, I'm going to share with you the different types of resilience that allow you to navigate uncertainty more effectively.

Natural resilience (according to *Positive Psychology*, Riopel 2019) is something you are born with and that comes naturally. Those with natural resilience are enthusiastic about life's experiences and are happy to play, learn and explore. Even if they get knocked down and taken off track, they do their best. One example of natural resilience is that of young children under the age of seven. Assuming they've not experienced any major trauma in life, children of this age typically have an abundant and inspiring approach to life.

Adaptive resilience, which can also be thought of as 'trial by fire', is developed when challenging circumstances force you to learn, change and adapt. Learning how to roll with life's punches can help you build resilience and grow stronger as a result.

Learned resilience is also known as restored resilience. It's important to observe and realise that you don't necessarily need to go through the same adverse event as your colleagues and yet you can still develop your resilience. You can learn techniques that help build resilience and, as a result, restore the natural resilience you had as a child.

Each of these are types of resilience that fill your resilience tank. Although it would be great to possess all three types, it's not always necessary. Greater amounts of resilience in one type can compensate for lower amounts in others. I would like you to reflect on this last point and consider this: what does your resilience tank look like?

As a leader, you must understand the different types of resilience, not only to help you navigate your way through situations but also to increase your self-awareness throughout the process. This is vital to taking your resilience to a level that enables you to perform consistently at your best most of the time.

Sources of resilience

Where does your resilience come from? It's not a singular attribute; it has four interconnected sources: emotional, social, mental and physical. Each source contributes uniquely to your overall capacity to cope and thrive.

Mental resilience refers to your ability to adapt to change and uncertainty. Leaders who possess this type of resilience are flexible and calm during times of crisis. They use mental strength to solve problems, move forward and remain purposeful even when they're facing setbacks.

Emotional resilience involves being able to regulate emotions during times of stress. Resilient leaders are aware of their emotional reactions and tend to be more connected to the self. Because of this, they're also able to calm their mind and manage their emotions when they're dealing with challenging experiences. Working on your emotional intelligence can have a positive effect on your emotional resilience.

Social resilience, also known as community resilience, involves the ability of groups or teams to recover from difficult situations, for example after an organisational restructuring or significant changes to the team such as a new leader or team member. Social resilience involves people connecting with others and working together to solve problems that affect people both individually and collectively.

Physical resilience relates to the body's ability to withstand and recover from physical challenges, stress or illness. Taking care of your physical wellbeing is essential for overall resilience and your ability to consistently perform at your peak as a leader.

Resilience enables you to respond to challenging situations and remain effective in the face of adversity. Difficult times can come in many forms, from economic downturns and natural disasters to personal crises or unexpected changes at work. No matter their source, you'll need resilience to face such challenges head on and not be overwhelmed by them. But you'll also need to tap into your resilience in times of success, a topic I'll cover later in this chapter.

A key aspect of resilience is having realistic expectations of yourself and others. Setting achievable yet challenging goals helps avoid frustration and demoralisation; striving for too much too soon can lead to burnout or disappointment if those goals aren't met quickly enough. Additionally, understanding other people's limitations, perhaps stemming from their own stress levels or skill set, will help you adjust your expectations accordingly, enabling tasks to be completed successfully within realistic boundaries and timelines.

How you react during difficult times will make all the difference between success and failure. Staying calm and composed no matter how intense the situation may become will allow you to continue functioning effectively while inspiring confidence in your team members and colleagues. Crucially, acknowledging weaknesses without viewing them as roadblocks also demonstrates emotional intelligence, as does the recognition that mistakes are learning opportunities rather than a cause for criticism or a reason for lack of progress overall.

Observations

Resilience can be summed up as feeling comfortable with the uncomfortable. There are no positive or negative emotions – there are just emotions. I want you to reflect on this before you read further or consider how you may develop or tap into your resilience. This is because human perception is extremely powerful and the way we interpret a situation drives our emotions and ultimately our behaviour.

Resilience develops through experience. However, that doesn't mean you must go through life-changing or traumatic experiences in order to develop it. How do you deal with unexpected events and how quickly do you move forward? If I have a meeting in the morning that goes badly and not at all how I was expecting, does it affect my next meeting? Does it affect lunchtime, the next day or even the next week? How quickly can I return to my optimum performance?

While there may be many other characteristics that you demonstrate as a resilient leader, from my own experience I'd say that the most important one is your ability to view change as a challenge or an opportunity. Also, it's about being acutely aware of the limits of control and actively practising letting go and self-efficacy – the unshakeable belief in your ability to succeed in any situation at any given time. Here are my top three observations about resilient leaders.

Observation #1: When it comes to success, they understand the importance of resilience

Many people associate resilience with recovering from some sort of adversity and that's where definitions of resilience tend to stop. But for high performers and senior leaders like you, that's not enough. Resilience may be perceived as a trait for getting you through adverse situations but you also need to be extremely resilient to deal with success.

Imagine you've always had ambitions to become a senior leader, to be promoted to a member of the organisation's C-suite. Navigating the recruitment process is politically complex. At this level, it's not about simply applying for the job and excelling at interview. It's a long and onerous process, fraught with challenges along the way. It takes resilience to complete that journey. Then, suddenly, you've secured the promotion you've been dreaming of and working hard for.

Your first job is to restructure, rebrand, create a new organisation or set up a new department. You're leading it and all eyes are on you. You're instigating change and the pressure is on. And you're not going to get much empathy from those around you, those who are still congratulating you and thinking you did wonderfully well. So you're feeling happy but the pressure that comes with being in the limelight, making the big, possibly unpopular decisions and bringing people with you is huge. Being trusted to deliver and perform requires the same resilience to move forward. Without it, you won't succeed.

The resilience that's required for success isn't a transient thing. It doesn't end with achieving your first big goal. There will be other goals to pursue. It can be compared with the resilience that an athlete needs to achieve an Olympic gold medal. It's a euphoric moment; the effort, drive and resilience have carried them through to the pinnacle of their sporting career. But when they go for that second or third gold medal, a very different level of resilience is required for success. It's almost expected of them. If they win, that's great, but it's just another medal. If they don't win, that becomes the focus of interest, raising questions about why they didn't win.

It's the same with senior leadership positions in the corporate world. Everybody is looking at you and expecting you to do amazing, incredible things straight away. But you need recovery time – not to recover from adversity but to recover from the emotional turmoil that comes with achieving your goal and dealing with the pressure of how you then move forward.

By now it should be clear that resilience is an indispensable quality, even when you're basking in the glow of success – but it's crucial to nurture this quality amid the triumph. Here's why. First and foremost, success is not a destination; it's an ongoing journey. You can't rest on your laurels or become complacent once you've achieved success. You must keep pushing forward, adapting to new challenges and growing with each passing day. Resilience is the bedrock that allows you to weather the storms, learn from failures and continually improve yourself.

Imagine you've reached the summit of triumph, and suddenly an unforeseen setback knocks you off course. It's in those moments that resilience shines at its brightest. It's the resilient souls who dust themselves off, learn from their stumbles and find the strength to forge ahead. They refuse to let setbacks define their future, instead transforming them into stepping stones towards even greater victories.

Success comes with its fair share of stress and pressure. The higher you climb, the greater the expectations and demands placed upon you. Resilience equips you with the mental fortitude to handle such pressures with grace. It keeps you centred, allowing you to make sound decisions amid the chaos, maintain a healthy work–

life integration and prevent burnout from casting its shadow on your path.

And let's not forget the power of growth and change. Success can breed complacency, where risks are shunned and growth stagnates. But true resilience rejects such stagnation, propelling you to embrace change, seize new opportunities and continuously evolve. It instils within you an unwavering hunger for knowledge, innovation and pushing beyond the boundaries of what's comfortable. As you ascend to great heights of accomplishment, others look up to you. You become a beacon of inspiration, a leader worth following. And in this role, resilience is your greatest gift to those around you. It showcases your indomitable spirit, encouraging others to rise above their own challenges, maintain a positive attitude and relentlessly pursue their dreams.

Next time you land a project or a role you've always wanted, closed long and difficult negotiations or have been nominated for an award, don't expect every moment to be joyful. Tap into your resilience to reach your potential and fulfil your own and others' expectations of you.

Observation #2: They continually strengthen their resilience muscle

The good news is that resilience can be developed. Even if you're not a naturally resilient person, you can learn to develop a resilient mindset and attitude. Thoughts and emotions emerging in times of uncertainty are better dealt with sooner than later. At this point, you must focus on what you can control and influence while relentlessly seeking an opportunity in every crisis because there will always be one.

Resilience lives outside your comfort zone and you can develop it but like any skill it must be practised. Therefore a step-by-step approach to gaining confidence and strengthening your so-called 'resilience muscle' is the key to success.

Reframe the way you think: This requires you to examine a situation or challenge from a different perspective and explore other reasons for what could be going on. Consider the possible benefits of the situation or whether you're missing something. For example, if a key member of the team suddenly resigns, the temptation may be to focus on the loss and the implications for the rest of the team. Alternatively, you can choose to reframe it as an opportunity to bring in new talent.

Actively seek opportunities outside your comfort zone: Organisational challenges present opportunities for leaders to strengthen their resolve. In turn, this helps them develop their resilience. Every time you find yourself having to navigate a crisis or resolve a problem you'll find some strength in it. Pick out insights from these situations that you can learn from and strengthen your resilience muscle.

Remind yourself that this is about feeling comfortable with the uncomfortable: Don't link this to the situation; remind yourself of the opportunity to grow and develop so you can push through.

Observe yourself: Write down your thoughts and emotions while being mindful that there are no positive or negative emotions and reflect on how these affect your behaviour and ability to deal with challenges.

Commit to continuous learning: You don't have to find the perfect response to every situation but learning from each experience and drawing on this knowledge base will increase your resilience over time.

Keep practising and don't judge yourself too harshly: Growth isn't easy and takes time. Developing your resilience is not a one-off exercise!

Resilience is nurtured by taking care of your physical, mental and emotional wellbeing. Maintain a balanced lifestyle that includes regular exercise, healthy eating, quality sleep and leisure activities that bring you joy. Take time for relaxation, self-reflection and engaging in activities that foster personal growth.

You may think that this all sounds wonderful but you don't have time for it. The choice is yours, however; self-care is not a luxury for leaders – it's a necessity for building resilience and leading effectively. By prioritising self-care practices such as setting boundaries, cultivating mindfulness, seeking support and mentorship, embracing physical wellbeing and learning from failure, you'll enhance your resilience and inspire those you lead.

Here are two practical examples of leaders who embraced self-care. John, a senior executive in the UK, embraced mindfulness as a self-care practice to enhance his resilience. He incorporated short mindfulness exercises into his daily routine, such as mindful breathing or taking a brief walk in nature, and developed greater self-awareness, improved his focus and gained a sense of calm amid the chaos. This allowed him to lead with clarity and make thoughtful decisions, even during challenging times.

Meanwhile, Sarah, the CEO of a tech firm in San Francisco, recognised the importance of setting boundaries to maintain her wellbeing. Despite her busy schedule, she prioritised carving out personal time for relaxation, hobbies and spending quality time with loved ones. By setting clear boundaries between her work and personal life, she preserved her energy and mental health, allowing her to show up as a resilient and balanced leader.

Over time, you'll become aware of your enhanced ability to deal more effectively with things that in the past created more challenges and to recover much faster and return to optimum performance. Developing resilience is a process, not an achievement.

Observation #3: They have a resilience routine

In order to tap into your resilience when required, you must develop a resilience routine, one that will be critical to your long-term success. I'm not talking about a one-off situation or surviving a lifetime event; I'm talking about successful, high-performance leadership that you can deliver day in and day out throughout your career. It's not a sprint, it's a marathon. You need to cultivate a tournament mentality. Your resilience routine starts with self-awareness, moves to self-acceptance and tapping into your leadership superpower, followed by reflection. Consistently repeating and practising this process allows you to cross the resilience bridge.

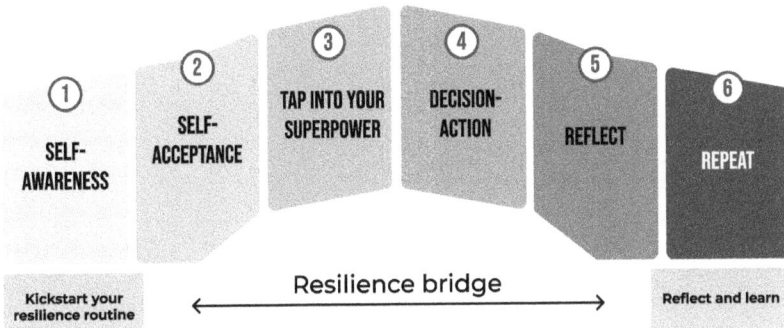

Figure 3: The resilience bridge

Self-awareness: By self-awareness, I don't mean awareness of yourself as an individual but an awareness of when it's time to tap into your resilience. How should I behave in this situation? What's the behaviour, the characteristic that will move me forward, because carrying on as things are isn't working? When you're finding things difficult and you feel uncomfortable, it's important to have the self-awareness to recognise what's happening.

Self-acceptance: You can't make progress with your resilience routine without accepting your situation and the reality that you're feeling uncomfortable and things are difficult. You'll remain where you are. Without acceptance, there's no real change in behaviour.

Tap into your leadership superpower: It's with self-acceptance that you start moving forward. At this stage you need to tap into your leadership superpower, that unique trait or skill that makes you exceptional. You can tap into it in many situations and use it to pivot your way out of them.

Decision and action: But you can't just stop and think, 'OK, now I know my superpower, I just need to use it.' You also need to make a decision about what you're going to do. What's the issue? What's the outcome you would like? Then it's time to move forward. If you haven't been able to take action, it is a clear sign that you haven't made a decision yet.

Reflect: This is a valuable checkpoint in your resilience routine. When you've made a decision about what you're going to do, don't just say you're going to do it; have a strategy about when you're going to do it and how you're going to measure its success. That's when you need to reflect. Is it working? Do I need to adjust it? This isn't a static or linear way of thinking – it's systematic thinking. Reflect and then repeat.

Repeat: Be on the lookout for opportunities to tap into your routine, because you need to practise, practise, practise to strengthen your resilience muscles and feel confident that you can be resilient when it matters.

I recently called on my own resilience routine to get through a crisis. In February 2020, if you'd asked me to deliver a one-week residential retreat or training course for your board members I couldn't have done it. I was fully booked for the entire year. Two weeks later, Covid-19 arrived and everything changed. I've faced many challenges as a business owner: overcoming cultural barriers, launching businesses in different countries and navigating recessions. So when news of the pandemic broke, I felt confident I could handle the situation. But then I started receiving emails from clients cancelling and postponing training sessions indefinitely. This had never happened to me before.

I spent a week observing the situation, asking myself how I felt (I was probably in shock) but also recognising that the longer I remained in this state of mind, the more delayed my reaction and action would be. My self-awareness was there but my self-acceptance didn't kick in until seven days later. The reality was that things weren't looking good. What was I going to do about it? My superpower is resilience but how was I going to use it in such a dire situation? That's when I took the decision to approach some of those customer cancellations and offer them an alternative. I'd been coaching overseas clients virtually for many years. Why not do it for everybody – redesign the programme and deliver it in a different way?

Some organisations weren't prepared for this innovative approach. This was a second shock for me. What do you do when you think you have a solution but others are not ready for it? I retraced some steps on my resilience curve to revisit 'What are you going to do?' Tapping into my resilience, I decided to launch a new virtual masterclass, specifically aimed at senior leaders who'd never had the experience or considered the concept of virtual training, coaching, learning, growing and developing.

Some gave in to the fear zone and wanted to wait until Covid-19 had passed. But waiting, high performance and resilience are not a good combination. Thankfully, others were willing to embrace change and within three months my courses were fully booked again. When I reflected on this, I realised it was my routine of resilience and understanding my superpower that prompted me into action and enabled me to pivot – and that being comfortable with being uncomfortable was the key to success.

It's important to remember that, as resilience expert and cognitive behavioural coach Michael Keenan pointed out, even after being knocked by something that has happened, the darkest times still typically lead to growth. Developing resilience can lead to a new or revised and enhanced self-image. It can also strengthen, enrich and clarify your relationships. You'll become aware of unexpected abilities as you rise to each new challenge. During difficult times, you'll also recognise the friends who remain and offer support and those who no longer return calls or are toxic or draining. You'll prioritise positive relationships. You'll also have a change of mindset when it comes to your priorities.

You still have to go through the fear zone, but your resilience will help you to expand and widen your comfort zone. Putting time into developing your resilience will ensure that it serves you well for many years.

REFLECT AND GROW

Here are the top three key takeaways from PRINCIPLE 3:

+ *Resilience is not about being tough – but it can be tough.*

+ *As a high-performance thinker, embracing resilience will give you a competitive advantage.*

+ *Create a resilience routine and don't forget to exercise your resilience muscle regularly to keep it in top shape.*

Reflect on the three points below:

+ *What does resilience mean to you and how do you tap into it?*

+ *Reflect on a leadership or life situation when your resilience was critical to success.*

+ *How has your perspective on resilience changed after reading this chapter?*

YOUR PERFORMANCE ADVANTAGE HACK

Resilience is often misunderstood. Share the concept of the resilience bridge with your team and your network. You can also ask them to consider the questions above as an opportunity to reflect and grow.

PRINCIPLE (4)

SUBTRACT COMPLEXITY TO ADD VALUE

Where focus goes, energy flows. – Tony Robbins

In today's complex, 'always on' world, it's easy to think that doing more, adding to your workload or staying longer in the office to answer one more email or call will deliver a better outcome. Leaders are often faced with complex challenges that require complex solutions. The prevailing wisdom has always been that the more complex the solution, the more effective it will be. I would challenge that. If you want to be a successful high-performing leader, you need to subtract complexity.

Over the years I've helped many executive clients learn how to subtract complexity to create a stronger, faster impact and increase efficiency and effectiveness while maximising their own and their team's energy, time and skill sets. Subtracting complexity is the process of simplifying processes, systems and procedures to remove unnecessary complications.

It doesn't require extra effort but it does require you to think differently. Subtracting complexity holds untapped potential for unlocking remarkable growth and success.

I can recall a pivotal moment in my career as a leadership coach when I witnessed first hand the transformative power of subtraction. It was a crisp November day when I ventured into the bustling headquarters of a rapidly growing software development company. Despite its impressive growth, this organisation found itself entangled in a web of missed deadlines and faltering communication. Little did they know that the solution to their problems lay in the art of subtraction.

On my arrival I was greeted by one of the directors, who had been anticipating a routine supplier meeting. Armed with a radically different proposal titled 'Subtract Complexity to Add Value', I unveiled a concept that would change the organisation's trajectory forever. From the initial briefing, it became evident that they had fallen prey to the pervasive inclination to accumulate more tasks and introduce more processes and therefore more complexity. Together with the team of directors, we embarked on a journey of subtraction that would revolutionise their way of thinking. The methodology got integrated into the organisation's culture and the way they do things. The impact was astounding. The company, once burdened by missed deadlines and diminishing innovation, was reinvigorated. They rediscovered their entrepreneurial spirit and rose to meet every challenge head on. The power of subtraction extended beyond the confines of operational efficiency. Employee engagement soared as team members were inspired and felt a renewed sense of purpose.

Subtracting complexity is just as important at a personal level as it is at the organisational one. For example, a big part of being a leader is learning how to manage your energy. No one has limitless amounts of energy, so deciding where to direct your focus and attention is crucial. It's a challenge because you're constantly being bombarded with messages via emails, messaging platforms and social media, all competing for your time and attention and ultimately impacting your leadership performance. Maximising your impact as a leader begins with regularly fine-tuning your prioritisation and decision-making skills. A clear understanding of what's urgent and what's important should be at the forefront of your mind. My aim in this chapter is to provide you with ways to navigate what I call the 'attention highway in rush hour' and to challenge you to focus your attention on subtracting complexity. I guarantee you'll be surprised at how much value you can add.

How to subtract complexity

Research has shown that, over time, internal complexity seems to gradually increase in most organisations. A study published in the journal *Nature* (Adams et al 2021) concluded that there's a cognitive bias known as subtraction neglect. As the name suggests, it leads people to add things and ignore the possibility of subtracting things to solve a problem. As a leader grappling with the challenges posed by ever-accelerating change, you may be well aware of this.

To remain competitive, organisations are increasingly embracing transformation and restructuring strategies. An integral component of these initiatives is the art of subtracting complexity, a process that entails simplifying processes and systems to eliminate unnecessary complications and enhance operational efficiency. I've accompanied many senior leaders on their journey to subtracting complexity through transformation and restructuring, ultimately adding value to their organisations. So what does it look like in practice? A key method of subtracting complexity involves a streamlining process – the meticulous analysis of existing workflows to identify redundancies, unnecessary steps and convoluted procedures. By eliminating these inefficiencies, you can unlock opportunities for optimisation, streamlining productivity and mitigating bottlenecks. Then, by applying automation and the strategic reorganisation of workflows, you can further reduce complexity, enhancing your organisation's operational effectiveness and use of resources.

Another key strategy in complexity subtraction is the simplification of organisational structures, flattening hierarchies, removing redundant roles or departments and empowering employees to make independent decisions. When you minimise bureaucracy and centralise decision-making authority, you're fostering a culture of agility and efficiency. A simplified structure improves decision making, encourages collaboration and facilitates a nimble and much more responsive organisation that's better able to adapt to dynamic market conditions.

Organisations are often burdened with a multitude of product or service offerings, inadvertently creating unnecessary complexity. You can address this challenge by undertaking a comprehensive review and rationalisation of these offerings. Focus on core products or services that align with your customer needs and strategic objectives. By narrowing the portfolio, your organisation can allocate resources more effectively, deliver value and improve profitability. The result will be a leaner and more focused business model that resonates with your customers and differentiates your organisation from your competitors.

Complexity can also result from the proliferation of disparate systems and technologies employed across various operational domains. An effective way to address this issue is to embrace system and technology consolidation, eliminating data silos, reducing redundancies and improving operational cohesion. Not only does this minimise complexity, but it also facilitates seamless information flow and better decision making and optimises cost structures. By taking this approach you can create a cohesive and efficient infrastructure that aligns with your organisation's strategic goals.

Subtracting complexity from your leadership

Leadership is often complex and demanding but what if the key to being more effective as a leader is actually subtracting from rather than adding more to your plate? How does this add value to your leadership? Most importantly, what does it look like?

Increased clarity: clarifying goals, priorities and actions, making it easier to communicate them to your team.

Better decision making: with fewer distractions and a clearer understanding of your goals, you can make more informed decisions that align with your vision and values.

Improved efficiency: you can streamline your processes and workflows, making it easier to get things done. This can improve your team's productivity and reduce the likelihood of burnout.

Increased innovation: free up mental bandwidth for creative thinking and innovation. This part of the process is often ignored but it's pivotal.

Enhanced adaptability: simplifying your approach can help you be more agile and responsive, making it easier to pivot and adjust to new challenges.

How to identify areas of complexity in your leadership

Reflect on your leadership style and consider areas where you may be overcomplicating things. Ask yourself these questions:

+ Am I micromanaging my team?
+ Am I taking on too many tasks?
+ Am I communicating effectively with my team?

Seek feedback from colleagues, mentors or members of your team to understand their perspectives on where you may be adding complexity. Ask for specific examples and try to be open to their feedback. Take a close look at your processes and workflows to identify areas where you might be adding unnecessary complexity. Are there too many steps in a particular process? Consider whether some can be eliminated or combined to increase simplicity. You may be using too many tools or systems. But don't overlook the fact that technology can be a powerful tool for simplifying your approach. Automation tools, collaboration software and project management software can streamline your workflows and make your work more efficient.

Communication is key to effective leadership but it can also be a source of complexity. Review your communication channels and consider whether you may be over-communicating or using too many channels.

Evaluate your workload and consider whether you may be taking on too much. Are you prioritising your tasks effectively? Simplify your workload by prioritising your tasks based on their importance and urgency. Eliminate tasks that are not essential to your goals or vision.

Use a tool such as a to-do list or project management software to free up your time and help you stay organised and focused on what matters most. However, simplifying your approach doesn't mean cutting corners or compromising; in fact, it means quite the opposite.

Are you delegating effectively? One of the most effective ways to simplify your approach is to delegate tasks to your team members. This will free up your time and mental bandwidth to focus on what's most important, while also empowering your team members to take ownership of their work.

I'd recommend that you regularly reflect on these aspects of simplifying your approach without compromising on the quality of your leadership. Many of my coaching clients use this as a checklist or a reminder to evaluate their performance. I challenge you to subtract. Embrace the simplicity that lies within the chaos.

Observations

I'm not a great fan of the term 'work–life balance'. Achieving balance suggests seeking perfection or chasing the impossible, setting yourself up for failure, stress and unnecessary complications. That puts additional pressure on you as a leader. What I'm a huge fan of is work–life integration, which means integrating your work into your life, not the other way around. You're helping yourself to think differently about your work and your life, developing better habits and consciously reducing the complexity around you.

At this stage, you may be thinking that although it all sounds good you're too busy and don't have time for it. Or you may have already tapped into the concept but haven't quite nailed it. Either way, I urge you to continue reading with an open mindset and the willingness to try new ways of working.

The way that we work has changed radically in recent times. Technology has transformed processes and practices, yet the fast pace of evolution in digital technologies and endless new systems are not always designed to simplify things. They can increase the level of complexity you face as a leader. Once you've identified the complexity in your leadership, it's time to put things into practice and subtract complexity from your thinking, feeling and behaviour.

Here are my top three observations on how high-performing leaders subtract complexity from their day-to-day responsibilities.

Observation #1: They expend most of their energy on things they can control and influence

Even if you're an experienced leader and have absolutely nailed your work–life integration, the potential for expending too much energy on things you can't control can quickly drain your battery and affect your overall performance. It will require mental discipline to navigate your thinking towards areas within your control and let go of the rest.

You undoubtedly have many responsibilities and some significant challenges, whether that means digital transformation projects, new product launches, takeovers, mergers or organisational restructuring. All of these will have multiple stakeholders who will all be trying to exert influence but the responsibility for leading this strategy ultimately rests with you, and it can feel overwhelming.

Accepting the idea that there are some things that you simply can't control can be profoundly liberating. It can help you let go of anxiety and stress and focus on the things that you can change. I recommend you spend time distinguishing between the things you can control and the things you can't. For example, your thoughts, emotions, reactions and actions are within your control, so these are the things you need to focus on and strive to improve. Outside your control are things such as other people's behaviours and their opinions of you, along with external factors such as the economy and random life events. These are also the things you don't want to waste energy worrying about.

In the diagram below, you'll see three concentric circles of different sizes. The first and smallest circle at the centre is the circle of control, representing those aspects of your life over which you have direct control and where you can effect change by taking meaningful action to make a positive impact. Try to focus most of your attention and energy on this circle. The more focus you put on the circle of control, the bigger it grows and the less room there is for focus on things that are out of your control.

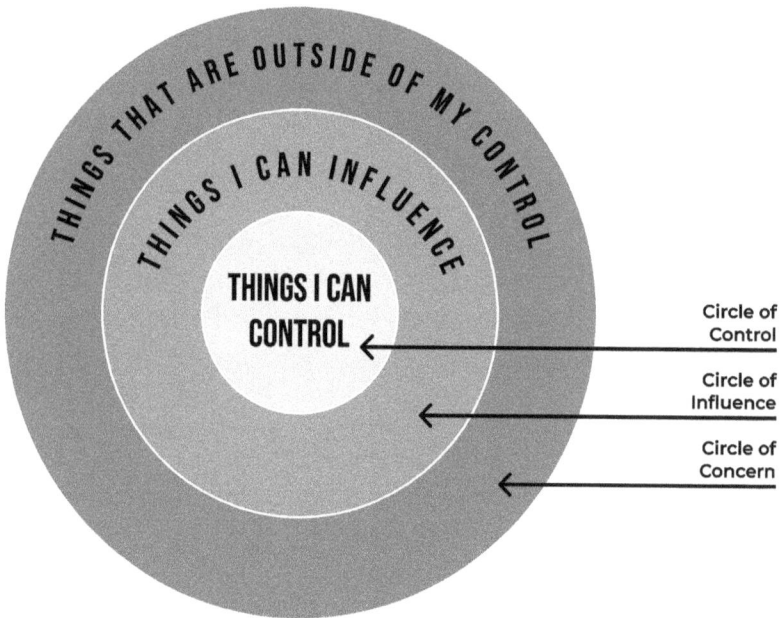

Figure 4: The circles of control

The second circle is the circle of influence, which represents the intersection of those things you can control and those that fall outside your area of control. You may not be able to exert your influence in this area but you can certainly try, so it's worth expending some of your energy in this circle. For example, you may not be able to directly control the behaviour of someone close to you but you can influence their behaviour by supporting and advising them.

The largest and outermost circle represents the circle of concern, encompassing those circumstances, events and other external factors that you might care about but have no control over.

Whenever you feel overwhelmed, stressed or unsure of how to move forward, simply grab a pen and paper, draw three circles and map out your thoughts. If you notice that you sometimes pay too much attention to the events in the circle of concern, try to directly engage with the items in the circle of control. The more energy you direct to the things you're in charge of, the more likely your life will align with your internalised goals and values.

You may not have seen this model before and could well be thinking 'I don't have time for this' or 'I have to turn my life upside down to do this'. But this isn't a burden or an extra task. I'm talking about tiny shifts, adopting a growth mindset, trying something different and seeing what happens and being agile and adaptable. Not even considering the concept of subtracting complexity is a missed opportunity.

For many leaders, their concern is about issues outside their control and influence and they simply ignore the other two zones. Remember, where focus goes, energy flows. Go back and look at what's in the control zone. I do this all the time. For example, in meetings, I'll draw three circles and identify what I'm in control of in this situation. Ask yourself what's in your mind that you need to know about. It's also about context. You can't, for example, control or change legislation. Equally, there will be targets for a task or project that have been agreed and you're unlikely to change. Instead, focus on the things you can influence and are in control of.

When you find yourself spending most of your time in the concerned zone, as we all do from time to time, that's the time to pause, reflect and pull back a little. Let me subtract some complexity here, because the complexity comes from the concern. When you spend a lot of time there, you're spending time and energy on things you can't control and in the meantime you're not spending time on things you can.

There will always be things beyond your control that can waste your precious time and energy. Use the circles of control to figure out what aspects of your life and business you don't have control over. Place these in the outer circle. This helps you to visually see the things that you can't control.

By focusing on the things that are within your control, you can take an active role in shaping your life and creating the outcomes that you desire. This will help you to feel more empowered and in control of your circumstances. On the other hand, trying to control things that are outside your control can be frustrating and ultimately futile, so it's important to recognise these limitations and stop worrying about things outside your inner circle.

One prominent figure who stands out for their remarkable ability to embrace the circle of control is Nelson Mandela. The legendary leader, who triumphed over adversity and transformed a nation, exemplified the wisdom of focusing on what one can control rather than being consumed by external factors.

Mandela endured decades of imprisonment for his fight against apartheid in South Africa. Throughout his confinement, he could easily have become disheartened, losing hope and dwelling on the circumstances beyond his control. However, he understood that his power lay in the choices he made within his sphere of influence. Even in the face of immense adversity, Mandela maintained an unwavering focus on his mission and the principles that guided him. He used his time in prison to educate himself, to deepen his understanding of the issues plaguing his country and to refine his vision for a united South Africa.

When Mandela finally emerged from prison and assumed the role of president, he faced the immense challenge of reconciling a divided nation. Yet Mandela chose to channel his energy towards the aspects he could control: his words, his actions and his unwavering commitment to forgiveness and reconciliation.

Mandela knew that he couldn't change the past or control the emotions and actions of others. However, he recognised that he could control his response to those circumstances. He chose to lead by example, demonstrating empathy and compassion even towards those who had oppressed him and his people.

Mandela's journey teaches us a profound leadership lesson: by focusing on what we can control, we unleash our true potential and inspire others to do the same. As leaders, we must resist the temptation to be consumed by external factors that are beyond our control. Instead, we should channel our energy towards what is within our influence – our attitudes, our actions and our ability to create positive change.

Observation #2: They prioritise with discipline

Although it can often appear that way, not everything is urgent or important. Prioritising isn't about picking the most important-looking item from your to-do list or dealing with an issue that a team member has just asked you to address.

Your brain is being continuously bombarded with information. In the age of hybrid and digital, the bombardment is even more intense, with less separation between work and home. All the more reason for subtracting complexity by doing things that will enhance your self-management capabilities.

Forget to-do lists and schedules and use blocks instead. My diary is built in blocks, chunks of time that I block out for focusing on particular tasks. I also block out time for thinking. Take emails, for example. I advise against constantly keeping your email inbox open. Though it might be tempting, this habit can prove detrimental and highly inefficient, as your entire day may be consumed by constant responses. Instead, a more sensible approach is to designate specific periods in the morning or evening – whichever suits your schedule best – and reserve those times for handling your emails. By doing so, you can maintain better focus and productivity while managing your inbox effectively.

If you're a leader, you have team meetings, you have your board participation, you have other meetings and you may also have to deal with recruitment. So while it's not always possible, blocking out certain parts of the day will help your brain to focus.

I also advocate using the Eisenhower matrix to prioritise: either deal with it, diarise it, delegate it or dump it. It was during a 1954 speech that former US President Dwight D Eisenhower, who was quoting Dr J. Roscoe Miller, president of Northwestern University, said, 'I have two kinds of problems: the urgent and the important. The urgent are not important, and the important are never urgent.' This is said to be how he organised his workload and priorities.

	HIGH URGENCY	LOW URGENCY
HIGH PRIORITY	① **DO FIRST** — Important task	② **DELAY** — Schedule to complete
LOW PRIORITY	③ **DELEGATE** — Can be done by someone else	④ **DON'T DO** — Distraction

Figure 5: The Eisenhower matrix

Whether they are professional or personal, important activities have an outcome that leads to the achievement of your goals. Urgent activities demand immediate attention and are usually associated with achieving someone else's goals. They're often the ones you concentrate on and they demand attention because the consequences of not dealing with them are immediate. However, when you're a senior leader you can't take someone else's priorities and make them your own because the basis and origins of their priorities will be very different to yours. Their level of responsibility is different. And this is where the boundaries are so critical.

If something is urgent and has to be done, then delegate it to someone else. Avoid jumping immediately into trying to do everything that needs doing, even though the impulse is huge. It's tempting to think 'I can solve this quickly', but how many such moments come your way in a day? If it's not urgent, not important, it's not the number one priority. Learn the power of 'not now' and 'not yet'! These are two of the most important phrases that you and your team need to learn.

I use the Eisenhower matrix all the time. In fact, I have it on a whiteboard in my office and use Post-it notes so that I can easily move and reallocate tasks. Let me share an example of how a tech CEO client makes use of the matrix to subtract complexity. Sanjay leads a fast-growing technology company but is constantly bombarded with a multitude of tasks, meetings and requests, making it challenging to maintain focus and achieve strategic goals. Recognising the need for prioritisation, Sanjay uses the Eisenhower matrix to categorise tasks based on their urgency and importance. Urgent tasks require immediate attention, while important tasks contribute significantly to long-term goals. With this clarity, Sanjay begins the process of prioritisation.

In the top-left quadrant of the matrix, Sanjay identifies tasks that are both urgent and important. These are critical matters that demand immediate attention and align with the company's strategic objectives. Addressing a major customer issue that could impact the company's reputation falls into this category. Sanjay swiftly takes action, allocating resources and personally intervening to resolve the issue promptly.

In the top-right quadrant, Sanjay identifies tasks that are important but not necessarily urgent. These are activities that contribute to long-term success but may not require immediate attention. For instance, developing a new product roadmap to stay ahead of market trends would fall into this quadrant. Sanjay recognises the significance of these tasks and sets aside dedicated time on the schedule to focus on them, ensuring they receive the attention they deserve.

In the bottom-left quadrant, Sanjay places tasks that are urgent but not important. These are typically distractions or low-priority requests that demand an immediate response but don't contribute significantly to long-term goals. Examples could include responding to non-essential emails or attending to minor administrative tasks.

To manage these efficiently, Sanjay delegates them to capable team members or allocates specific time slots to address them quickly, minimising their impact on more important activities.

In the bottom-right quadrant, Sanjay identifies tasks that are neither urgent nor important. These tasks are generally time-wasters or unnecessary activities that provide minimal value. They should be minimised or eliminated whenever possible. For instance, attending non-essential meetings or spending excessive time on social media fall into this category. Sanjay consciously avoids or delegates these tasks, freeing up time for more important responsibilities.

By employing the Eisenhower matrix, Sanjay gains clarity and focuses on high-priority tasks that align with the company's strategic objectives. This approach allows Sanjay to make better decisions regarding resource allocation, time management and personal involvement, leading to increased productivity and progress towards the organisation's goals. And by avoiding or eliminating tasks that are neither urgent nor important, Sanjay optimises time and energy for more valuable endeavours.

Observation #3: They have mastered the art of decision making

As a leader, making decisions is your job, your responsibility, your life but you're often making them without having all the relevant information available to you. How much information is enough? How much is good enough? This brings us to the question of your style of decision making: do you strive for 'good enough' or 'the very best'? Is it focused on maximising or satisfying? In his book *The Paradox of Choice* (2004), Barry Schwartz distinguishes between two kinds of deliberators – maximisers and 'satisficers'. Both carefully consider their decisions but in different ways.

Maximisers will accept only the best possible option. Individuals who employ this style aim to optimise or maximise their returns by making the best decisions possible. They attempt to embody the ideal of the rational chooser through an extended decision process, making decisions based on rationality and logical reasoning. According to this ideal, a rational decision maker carefully weighs all available information, considers potential outcomes and consequences and chooses the option that best achieves their objectives. The phrase 'through an extended decision process' indicates that these individuals invest considerable time and effort in making decisions. They may gather extensive information, analyse various alternatives and deliberate at length before arriving at a conclusion. By engaging in such an extended process, they seek to make well-informed and carefully considered choices.

Satisficers (a term that combines the words 'satisfy' and 'suffice' and was coined by American psychologist Herbert Simon in the 1950s) are individuals who accept an option that meets their standards. According to his research (1955), individuals who employ this style tend to focus on making the first acceptable choice rather than the best one. In other words, satisficers are more likely to accept the first satisfactory or sufficient solution than continue to weigh up options in search of the optimal one.

One approach that I think is particularly helpful in these situations is to simplify decision making not by focusing on the outcome but on the goal of the decision. Many leaders approach decision making by identifying a solution. With that fixed outcome in mind, they then have to deal with the complexities of reaching that predefined solution. Instead, consider what you want to achieve with your decision:

+ Do you want to maximise accuracy?
+ Do you want to maximise transparency?
+ Do you want to minimise effort?
+ Do you want to minimise emotional strain?

The key thing is to set only one decision goal. This will help you subtract complexity from the decision-making process.

A decision is nothing more than a combination of judgement and bias. So how do you make decisions when everybody wants different things from you? Every stakeholder is making demands of you, your team is chasing you for certain things, the documents are saying something else and the pressure is building. Choose your decision goal wisely.

If you find yourself getting stuck or blocked, instead of concentrating on the outcome or solution, focus on how you make a decision. Allow the decision goals to move you forward. Subtracting complexity is a process that allows you to think differently, free up your mind, and most importantly, move forward on your leadership journey.

I recently had the privilege of facilitating a board retreat for a members-only association. The organisation's board members and management team were grappling with a strategic decision-making dilemma concerning the most effective growth strategy for the association.

Upon my arrival, they eagerly presented their three meticulously crafted strategic options. However, it required some persuasion and trust-building on my part to convince them that we needed to thoroughly evaluate these options. My primary objective was to help them comprehend their decision-making styles and emphasise the importance of establishing a clear decision goal. My intention was to guide them towards unlocking their untapped thinking potential and overcoming their current impasse. Through a brief exercise, it became apparent that the management team predominantly comprised maximisers rather than satisficers. When I inquired about their decision goal, they seemed puzzled. Following on, they unanimously opted for accuracy as the decision goal. However, after a short ideation session, the team collectively realised that board transparency was crucial for presenting the strategic options to the members during the upcoming annual general meeting. This changed the game and subtracted complexity from their long, drawn-out process. Incredibly, after a four-hour retreat they were able to move forward despite having been stuck with strategic options for some months.

REFLECT AND GROW

Here are the top three key takeaways from PRINCIPLE 4:

+ *Learn to navigate the 'attention highway in rush hour'. If you're serious about adding value, focus your attention on subtracting complexity.*

+ *If you master the art of prioritising and decision making you'll be well on the way to high-performance leadership.*

+ *Be deliberate about what you focus on and mindful of the energy you dedicate to things outside your control and influence because nobody has endless energy, not even high-performing leaders.*

Reflect on the three points below:

+ *Identify ways in which you already subtract complexity to add value.*

+ *What area of your leadership would benefit further from the concept?*

+ *How will you use the circles of control and the Eisenhower matrix to add value by subtracting complexity?*

YOUR PERFORMANCE ADVANTAGE HACK

Take this concept to the team and organisation level. What area of your team and organisation would benefit further from subtracting complexity?

PART 2

NEXT LEVEL LEADERSHIP

PRINCIPLE 5

NAVIGATE YOUR LEADERSHIP JOURNEY

A leader knows the way, goes the way, and shows the way. –
John C. Maxwell

Your leadership is a journey, not a destination, and the journey itself is your ultimate reward. In a world fixated on achievement, it's easy to overlook the transformative power and fulfilment that lie within the process of leadership. Viewing your leadership as a journey will transform the way in which you perceive and approach it. It's a small but significant shift in your perspective that will elevate your performance and take success to a whole new level. Please don't see leadership as a checkbox to be ticked off or a one size fits all destination that follows a predetermined roadmap. See it as a multi-dimensional and ever-evolving expedition that demands continuous self-reflection, adaptability and growth.

When was the last time you mapped out your journey as a leader? I'm not talking about job titles or responsibilities but how, as a leader, you have changed, grown and transformed over the years. That journey didn't begin with your first leadership role or position. Think back to the first time you demonstrated leadership behaviour, perhaps at school or university, in your local community or within your family. Think about the significant pivotal points and ask yourself these questions:

+ How did your behaviour change?
+ How did your thinking change?
+ How have your feelings about leadership changed over time?

+ What does leadership even mean to you?
+ Why did you choose to become a leader and what motivates you to continue on this journey?
+ How do you want to continue your journey now?

I can distinctly recall the day that someone first called me a leader. At the age of 14, while living in a communist country and before the internet, I resorted to what you and I would call primary research on the topic. I asked my grandparents, talked to my great-uncle (who ran a restaurant and was a great source of information) and turned to five trusted teachers at my school. I concluded that a leader is a person who can influence others in some way. What shocked me, however, was the absence of any professional qualification that states that you're now a leader.

My curiosity piqued, I began my lifelong passion for observing others so that I could determine whether or not they were leaders. I also quickly realised that it wasn't as black and white as that. Slowly the answer began to crystallise that 'leader' is not a title you achieve but a behaviour you demonstrate that's present in all walks of life, including in Matraterenye, the rural Hungarian village where I grew up. I saw it in my great-uncle and my grandparents, who both led teams and were highly respected in the local community. But my years of study and immersion in the topic of leadership have taught me that it's not a one-off occurrence, which was contrary to what I thought as a youngster.

What does the journey of the leaders I coach or train look like? You may be surprised to hear that regardless of industry, sector and even national and geopolitical differences, many of the leaders I work with could be described as being on an expedition to K2. So at this stage of your career I want you to envisage your leadership journey in a similar way.

You may be somewhere between the third and fourth camp or on your way to the summit. You have acclimatised and are ready to embrace the next part of your journey. Bear in mind that many never attempt it at all. A few make it to several of the camps on the way, but even fewer make it to the summit. If you draw parallels with your leadership journey, where you are today is somewhere between the last two camps and the summit. Reaching the top requires a different way of thinking. Progress might be slower; there are lots of tiny steps, and every single step has to be precise and specific to the purpose. Some steps might be sidesteps. It's a much slower process than the steps you took earlier but you need to be extremely aware of the environment and the conditions all the time.

You have the choice of making this journey without oxygen or significantly accelerating your progress and increasing your chances of success by using sufficient oxygen, which I equate to embracing the power of high-performance thinking and PRINCIPLES 1 to 4. You may also decide to call upon the guidance of a Sherpa, which is similar to having a performance coach who has accompanied many on their leadership success journeys.

This is where high performers and successful leaders start but certainly don't stop. Your thinking is engaged and you know you can build on your superpower. You know how to exercise your resilience muscle and you've mastered subtracting complexity. You're perfectly positioned to map your leadership growth and your journey ahead. I want you to visualise your leadership as an ongoing voyage of self-discovery and personal development. Like a ship sailing across uncharted waters, leadership presents you with countless opportunities to explore your strengths, face your limitations and grow into the best version of yourself. So let's go.

Your leadership path

I urge you to see your leadership journey as an opportunity for continuous growth and evolution, enabling you to inspire and empower those around you. It's a topic that has been widely written about. In his book *On Becoming a Leader* (2009), Warren Bennis discusses the idea that rather than being a fixed set of skills or attributes, effective leadership is a journey of self-discovery and personal growth. In *Leaders Eat Last* (2014), Simon Sinek emphasises that leadership is a journey of service to others and that effective leaders are committed to lifelong learning and improvement. He also discusses the leadership journey from the perspective of creating a culture of trust and collaboration within organisations. He highlights the importance of selflessness, empathy and service to others as key principles for leaders who want to build strong teams and leave a positive legacy, which I invite you to reflect on.

High-performing leaders visualise their leadership journey as a path. It's not a fixed destination but rather a continuous journey of learning, growth and self-discovery that requires ongoing effort and commitment.

Take a minute to draw your leadership journey. When I set this task during my training sessions, most participants emerge with an upward curve. Some may consider the option of a series of bendy roads. If you've done the same, don't worry; this is what most leadership courses have taught us but in reality, especially at senior level, the map looks very different, and this is why.

Visualise the map of your leadership journey as a forest with multiple paths. Some are smooth, some are uneven. There will be obstacles on the paths, such as fallen trees. Some paths are invisible until you set foot on them. At this stage of your career, there's nothing linear about your journey, even though it may have been previously.

And in this world of paths, you always have the option of switching paths in order to continue on the leadership journey you've mapped out. While you've developed the capability, you're leading more people and have bigger budgets. Your success is no longer about adding to these tangible milestones; it's about making conscious decisions about which path to take.

It's never too soon or too late to map out your leadership journey. Think of leadership as a behaviour rather than a specific style and while you can take inspiration from different styles and theories, you need to focus on constructing a journey that is authentic to you.

I want you to visualise your leadership journey as a:

+ **path of self-discovery**. Leaders often see their leadership path as a journey of self-discovery, where they learn more about themselves and how they can best lead others.

+ **path of continuous learning and growth**. Leaders see their leadership path as a journey of ongoing development, where they continually seek out new knowledge and skills to improve their performance.

+ **path of responsibility**. They see leadership as a means to an end, rather than an end in itself. Your leadership journey is your reward.

Why should you think of leadership as a journey?

When leaders view leadership as a destination or a major achievement, they tend to focus on short-term goals and objectives or the title, power and authority that comes with the position. You must avoid this approach, as it's more likely to encourage you to take a narrow-minded view of leadership that revolves around maintaining the status quo and preserving your power. It will limit your ability to innovate, adapt and inspire your teams to achieve higher levels of performance.

When you see your leadership as a journey you develop a growth mindset that significantly enhances your personal and professional development. Therefore you need to recognise leadership as a process that involves continuous learning, feedback and self-reflection. When you view it as a journey, you become more receptive to new ideas, perspectives and approaches that will help you and your teams achieve your collective goals.

By visualising your journey you also acknowledge the importance of establishing relationships and networks. When all you can envisage is the destination, you're more inclined to focus on your own goals and objectives, often at the expense of those of your teams and colleagues. Having a clear leadership journey brings the importance of building strong relationships with your teams and stakeholders into sharp focus. When you invest time and energy into developing trust, respect and rapport with others, knowing that these relationships are critical to their success as well as the success of the organisation, you'll become a more impactful and effective leader. You'll also become more adaptable and agile. Focusing solely on your destination can leave you set in your ways and resistant to change, perceiving that it will undermine your authority or status. By focusing on your journey, you'll actively embrace change as an opportunity to learn, grow, improve, take risks, try new approaches and learn from failures and setbacks.

In visualising your leadership as a journey, you'll recognise one very important fact – that leadership is not a solo endeavour. No leader can achieve success alone. You need to build strong teams that are aligned with your vision, mission and values and empower those teams to take ownership of their work and develop their own leadership skills. With your journey mindset you will recognise more clearly the importance of building a culture of learning, growth and continuous improvement that involves everyone in the organisation.

Finally, with the leadership journey mindset comes the recognition that leadership isn't just about achieving results but also about leaving a legacy, investing in developing the next generation of leaders, building sustainable systems and processes and leaving a positive mark on your organisation and the wider community.

Observations

I'm sure you'll agree that your leadership is not simply a title or a position; it's a way of being and a calling to inspire, guide and empower others. Much like any journey worth taking, your leadership is characterised by the unknown and it's in these uncharted territories where your greatest growth and learning will unfold.

Without exception, successful leaders are intentional and purposeful in mapping out their leadership journey. It's not a one-time event but an agile, ongoing process of growth and development that unfolds as you reflect and identify where you are at any given moment. By continuously assessing your progress and making adjustments along the way you're maximising your potential as a leader and increasing your potential for long-term success.

Looking at your leadership journey is vital to your success because it helps you to focus on the journey rather than just the destination. When you focus solely on the end result, you can become impatient, stressed and may even compromise your values or integrity to achieve that result. However, when you focus on the process of getting to your destination, you're more likely to make better decisions, build stronger relationships and achieve sustainable success.

Leadership is not just about achieving a particular goal but also about the way that you get there. It involves building trust, inspiring and motivating others and creating a positive and productive work culture. By focusing on your leadership, you can improve your skills and become a better leader, which in turn will lead to better outcomes and a stronger team.

Even when you've reached a particular goal, there will always be new challenges to face and new opportunities to take advantage of. By focusing on your leadership journey you'll be better equipped to navigate these challenges more effectively. Here's the behaviour I observe in high-performing leaders.

Observation #1: They have a clear leadership purpose and philosophy

The first step on your leadership journey must be taken with a strong sense of purpose and vision. Successful leaders are driven by a desire to make a difference in the world and have a clear idea of what they want to achieve. Having this sense of purpose is key to having the motivation and determination to overcome the obstacles and setbacks you'll encounter along the way.

High-performing leaders take consistent actions and have clearly defined leadership philosophies, and by this I mean the beliefs, principles and sentiments that they use to lead their organisations and their people. It's this personal leadership philosophy that will keep you on course and guide you when you need to evaluate information and react during various situations and to various people.

Having a clear purpose and philosophy as a leader is critical to gaining the trust and respect of those you lead. It helps to establish a clear direction for your team, providing everyone with a common goal to work towards, which helps to align everyone's efforts towards achieving the same objective. For example, a CEO who believes in customer satisfaction as their core philosophy will ensure that all their employees prioritise the needs and preferences of their customers.

It's important to regularly reflect, revise and then share your purpose and philosophy as a leader. These are the five steps of the pathway that you should follow:

1. **Reflect on your experiences:** Take time to reflect on your leadership experiences and identify the moments when you felt most fulfilled and impactful as a leader. What were the circumstances that led to those experiences? What values and principles guided your decisions and actions? This reflection can help you identify the themes and values that are most important to you as a leader.

2. **Define your values:** Identify the values that are most important to you as a leader. These values should be the foundation of your leadership philosophy and guide your decision making and behaviour. Examples of values include integrity, accountability, transparency, empathy and innovation.

3. **Develop a mission statement:** Create a mission statement that defines your leadership purpose and vision. This statement should reflect your values and capture the impact that you want to make as a leader. Your mission statement can be simple and concise, such as 'to inspire and empower others to reach their full potential'.

4. **Align your actions with your philosophy:** Once you've defined your leadership purpose and philosophy, you must align your actions with your values. This means making decisions that are consistent with your mission statement and ensuring that your behaviour is in line with your values.

5. **Continuously evaluate and refine:** Your leadership purpose and philosophy should be dynamic and evolve. It's important to continually evaluate and refine your values and mission statement as you gain new experiences and insights. This can help you stay focused on your goals and ensure that your leadership remains relevant and impactful.

All of this will allow you to create a clear roadmap for achieving your leadership goals and making a positive impact in your organisation and community. As you navigate the intricate leadership landscape, remember that clear leadership philosophy and purpose are the bedrock of your success. They provide you with the clarity, focus and resilience needed to overcome challenges and inspire greatness in others. Embrace your philosophy with confidence, infuse your actions with purpose and watch as you unleash the true power within you.

Part of my role as a leadership coach and trainer is to guide and support clients on this extraordinary journey. Regardless of how experienced you are, it's unrealistic to expect you to come up with a leadership purpose and philosophy on your own. Therefore I always start by using the steps I shared with you earlier. That's when the magic happens, and seeing clients use their purpose and philosophy to share their own leadership journey and impact their organisation's success is something that I never grow tired of.

A few years ago, I was privileged to work closely with Antonio, a senior leader at an international intergovernmental organisation, who embraced a leadership philosophy centred around empowering through servant leadership. He believed that by serving and enabling his team members, he could create a culture where individuals felt valued, inspired and motivated. His purpose was to foster a culture of trust, growth and collaboration, ultimately leading to remarkable results. Antonio's leadership philosophy and purpose had a transformative impact on the success of his organisation and the partnerships they had engaged in at the time.

What did it all look like in practice? Trust was at the core of Antonio's leadership philosophy. He believed in building strong relationships based on transparency, integrity and mutual respect. By consistently demonstrating these qualities, he fostered an environment in which trust thrived. This trust formed the foundation for effective collaboration, open dialogue and risk taking, leading to innovative solutions and breakthrough ideas.

As with many of the great leaders I know, Antonio did not simply expect everyone to behave in a certain way just because he said so. He provided ample opportunities for learning, skill building and career advancement and recognised his team's unique talents and aspirations, actively supporting them in their personal and professional growth journeys. This investment in their development not only enhanced individual capabilities but also created a strong sense of loyalty and commitment to the organisation's mission and mandate.

Under Antonio's leadership, collaboration became a cornerstone of his organisation's culture. He fostered a collaborative environment by breaking down silos, promoting cross-functional teamwork and creating spaces for ideation and knowledge exchange. By encouraging diverse perspectives and nurturing a sense of collective purpose, he harnessed the power of collaboration to drive innovation, efficiency and success. By embracing his leadership purpose and philosophy, Antonio has not only created a transformational impact in his organisation but has also boosted his leadership success by being headhunted and offered a senior position at HQ. Today he's making a global impact.

Before you read on, I'd like you to reflect on Antonio's story and consider how your leadership purpose and philosophy have shaped your leadership journey so far. Is it time for you to revisit this topic?

Observation #2: They are clear about their leadership legacy

As a leader, you have a profound responsibility to recognise and embrace the inherent rewards found within the journey itself. It's this shift in focus that will allow you to transcend the allure of short-term accomplishments and instead focus on your lasting legacy.

During discovery calls before starting a coaching programme or during executive training sessions, I often ask leaders about their legacy. Their responses generally fall into three categories. The majority believe that it's something to think of at the end of their career. Others haven't even considered the concept of legacy or its importance for their leadership success. However, some have a clearly defined legacy and have known what they want their legacy to be from an early stage in their leadership journey. It's an important part of the mapping process for your leadership success journey.

You're never too young to decide what you want your legacy to be or to think about which path will ensure that you fulfil that legacy. One thing is for sure, though – if you wait until the end of your career you'll have left it too late. People often think of their legacy as a tangible, physical thing; for example, writing a book, developing a game-changing new product or founding a business. Those are legacies but they are left for other people. I'm talking about your leadership legacy, which can be something as simple as being kind.

I'm passionate about making leaders think differently so they can reach their full potential and create more leaders. That's my legacy. Your leadership legacy is for you. Defining a legacy will help you to clarify your vision and your goals and align your actions with your values. This allows you to focus on long-term results rather than short-term gains and leave a lasting impact on your organisation, community and potentially the world.

Your leadership legacy is important for a number of reasons:

+ **Providing direction:** Defining a legacy gives you a clear direction to follow and helps you stay focused on your goals and priorities. This will be especially important during times of uncertainty or crisis, when it may be difficult to make decisions without a clear sense of purpose.

✦ **Inspiring others:** When you're clear about your legacy, it can inspire and motivate others to join you in achieving goals. A clear vision and purpose create a sense of shared purpose and enthusiasm and helps to build a strong team culture.

✦ **Building credibility:** With a clearly defined legacy you can build credibility and trust with your followers. And when you consistently demonstrate your commitment to your values and goals, you'll establish a track record of success that enhances your reputation and influence.

✦ **Leaving a lasting impact:** Defining your legacy enables you to leave a lasting impact on your organisation. By creating a clear vision and taking action to achieve it, you'll make a positive difference that will be remembered long after you have moved on.

When I received a message from Ibrahim saying 'I'm not sure what to do; I don't think my legacy is good enough', I realised that he was doing his homework and falling prey to the misconceptions that often surround legacy – that it has to be unique, extraordinary and special. Yes, it has to be all that for you but it doesn't have to be audacious, nor does it need to sound world changing.

Ibrahim was a participant in one of my leadership inner circles programmes, which gave him the opportunity to engage on this topic with other participants and see how they were managing this task. At this point it was important to be vulnerable and share a bit more about my own legacy. Professionally, I like to make leaders think differently, and personally, I'd like to think I've made everyone feel special and valued, regardless of their education, background and expertise.

After sharing my thoughts, five minutes later I received another message from Ibrahim saying, 'Now I've got it. This is incredibly empowering for me. I'm so grateful to discover the power of legacy now and not even later in my career. It would have been such a missed opportunity. I'm going to tell everyone I know. This will definitely shape my leadership journey.'

Receiving messages like these makes me realise how I create impact and how defining and sharing my legacy continues to shape my own and others' leadership journeys. It also makes me appreciate my amazing clients.

Observation #3: They see their leadership journey as a pathway of opportunities

One important aspect of your leadership journey is the ability to identify and seize opportunities. For this, you need a keen sense of awareness, a willingness to take risks and the ability to adapt to changing circumstances. A major factor in your success as a leader rests on your ability to identify emerging trends and market opportunities and quickly pivot to capitalise on them.

Every decision you make about your leadership creates a new pathway of opportunities. This may be an opportunity to challenge yourself, grow or take on more responsibility. The path may be smooth or it may be uneven, but above all your leadership success journey is a pathway of opportunities that requires a combination of strategic thinking, relationship building and continuous learning.

All successful leaders have been on a unique and inspiring journey that has led them to where they are today. So rather than seeing it as a series of setbacks and challenges, view your journey to success as a pathway where each experience, challenge and setback presents a chance to learn and grow as an individual. This mindset will enable you to approach leadership with a sense of optimism and resilience and view obstacles as stepping stones rather than roadblocks.

There's no other way to say this – your leadership journey is not a meandering stroll through a tranquil garden but an exhilarating adventure full of challenges, triumphs and unexpected turns. It's time to shed the restraints of conventional thinking and perceive your journey as a dynamic network of opportunities. Each step you take presents a chance to grow, master resilience and elevate your leadership ability.

All too often I've seen leaders with huge potential who for some reason fail to perform or meet their own and others' expectations. When I share with them the concept of seeing leadership as a pathway of opportunities, I'm often met with a curious but somewhat wide-eyed look that tells me, 'I trust your expertise, Agnes, but can you please share an example of how it looks in practice?' And I can, via the extraordinary story of Hanne, an enterprising leader in the world of finance whom I first met at a conference in Frankfurt and have kept in touch with ever since.

Hanne encountered formidable obstacles on her path, from economic downturns to disruptive market forces. However, it was her unyielding belief in the inherent potential of opportunities that propelled her to unprecedented heights. She refused to succumb to adversity, recognising that setbacks were not stumbling blocks but pivotal moments for breakthroughs. Instead of wallowing in defeat, she channelled her energy into reimagining strategies, fostering innovation and challenging the status quo. By embracing setbacks as catalysts for growth, Hanne transformed adversity into a springboard for success, ultimately propelling her team to new heights of achievement.

Moreover, Hanne never settled for complacency. She possessed an insatiable thirst for knowledge, constantly seeking learning experiences to expand her expertise and sharpen her leading edge. She devoured industry research and leadership books, actively seeking out mentors who would challenge her thinking. By immersing herself in the relentless pursuit of growth, Hanne fortified her leadership acumen and forged a reputation as a visionary in her field.

Hanne's unwavering commitment to embracing opportunities also manifested in her approach to collaboration. She saw every interaction as a chance to forge powerful alliances, leverage collective wisdom and ignite synergies. By cultivating a strong network of allies, mentors and collaborators, Hanne tapped into an immense reservoir of knowledge, support and strategic partnerships. This collaborative spirit not only fuelled innovation but also empowered her team to surpass their limitations and achieve extraordinary outcomes.

As your leadership coach, I urge you to embrace Hanne's audacious mindset, one that views your leadership journey as a pathway of bold opportunities. Embrace each twist, each turn and each crossroads with unyielding determination and an unwavering belief in your ability to seize them for growth and transformation. Embrace these challenges as invitations to innovate fearlessly and become a catalyst for extraordinary change.

To adopt this audacious mindset with confidence and conviction, consider the following actions.

+ **Cultivate a growth mindset:** Embrace challenges as stepping stones to growth and development. Build resilience, adaptability and an unquenchable thirst for continuous improvement.

+ **Seek learning experiences:** Actively pursue learning opportunities that expand your knowledge, sharpen your skills and challenge your perspectives. Attend conferences, enrol in training programmes and consume relevant content to stay at the forefront of your industry.

+ **Embrace collaborative power:** Foster relationships with ambitious and like-minded individuals who complement your strengths and challenge your thinking. Engage in mentorship programmes, establish a robust professional network and nurture a culture of collaboration within your team.

+ **Reframe setbacks:** Reject the notion of setbacks as failures and reframe them as pivotal moments for learning and growth. Encourage your team to embrace a direct and bold approach to setbacks, extracting valuable lessons and leveraging them for future success.

Remember that your journey isn't defined by destinations but by the audacious strides you take along the way. Embrace the pathway of opportunities, for within its twists and turns lie the keys to unlocking your true leadership potential. Embrace the challenges with fierce determination, seek growth in every encounter and let your resolute leadership shine. Your journey awaits. Embrace it, seize the opportunities and become the fearless architect of your own greatness. We never actually arrive at the destination of being the best leader that we can be. It's something that we can aspire to, but this vision is always ahead of us as our leadership journey continues.

REFLECT AND GROW

Here are the top three key takeaways from PRINCIPLE 5:

+ *Leadership is a journey, not a destination and the journey is your reward, so it does matter how you choose to experience it. Stay true to your key leadership purpose and philosophy all the way.*

+ *If you're serious about making a lasting impact and being a successful, high-performing leader, don't wait to define your legacy. If you haven't done it already, do it now.*

+ *See your leadership success journey as a path of opportunities that you consciously choose.*

Reflect on the three points below:

+ *How will you keep the notion of the leadership success journey at the forefront of your and your team's minds when you're bombarded daily with demands for short-term achievements?*

+ *How will you incorporate high-performance thinking into your own, your team's and your organisation's leadership practice?*

+ *Who will you take on the journey with you to maximise your success and your potential? Peers, trusted individuals, your coach?*

YOUR PERFORMANCE ADVANTAGE HACK

Take time, perhaps 15–30 minutes, to regularly reflect on and map your leadership success journey. I'd expect you, as a high-performing senior leader, to do this every six months to stay ahead of the game and maximise your success. Don't forget that you're operating in a highly competitive environment where nobody waits for you or sets your leadership journey.

PRINCIPLE (6)

MASTER SELF-LEADERSHIP

It is not the mountain we conquer but ourselves. – attributed to Sir Edmund Hillary

Without you, there is no leadership. If you can't understand and lead yourself, then it's difficult to understand and lead others. When was the last time you reflected on your self-leadership? I want you to be honest with yourself because self-leadership starts with self-awareness but it doesn't stop there. Until you accept who you are, how you lead, how you think and who you are as a leader you won't fulfil your leadership potential and take your self-growth to the next level.

My life changed forever on 22 July 2006. I thought it was one of those weird dreams that feel scarily realistic but in this case it was my new reality. I had suddenly lost the sight in my right eye. It turned out that I'd had a stroke, with no prognosis and no prospect of when or if my sight would return. Shortly afterwards I also found out that I was pregnant. While I consider myself to be fairly resilient, it took me a while to adapt to this new reality.

In spite of everything, I was happy about the prospect of becoming a mum and put all my energy and focus into that. Ambitiously, six weeks later I attended my first public speaking event and things seemed to be going well. Then, one day, on my way to Guildford Eye Clinic, I called into a Waterstones bookshop. As I entered the store there was a huge collision. I didn't know what had happened; being partially sighted, what you don't see, you don't realise exists. It quickly became apparent that I'd walked into a gentleman with full force. He turned to me and said, 'Are you blind?' I looked at him and, with tears in my eyes, replied, 'Yes, I am.' Of course, he apologised profusely, but it was then that I realised I had to take ownership of this new reality. I had to step up and lead myself through the journey of recovery and acceptance, because I'd soon be a mother and without me there would be no business. I challenged myself and took my self-leadership to the next level. I had to embrace my journey and let go of my fears. And on 16 March 2007, I took up a new role in life – mum to my son Max – and I've never looked back.

You can probably understand and appreciate why I place great emphasis on the critical phase of self-discovery at the onset of every coaching engagement and why I've made self-leadership an integral component of my executive programmes, mastermind groups and leadership inner circle programmes. I'm deeply passionate about this topic and its profound impact on personal and professional growth. However, it appears that I have a bit more work to do, as it's still not uncommon for course participants and clients to seek clarification, asking 'What exactly do you mean by self-leadership?'

Within the scope of a coaching relationship, self-leadership serves as a foundation. It's a fundamental module that brings all aspects of my work together, providing guidance and direction to my clients' journeys towards achieving exceptional leadership outcomes. Defined as the ability to take charge of one's life, thoughts, emotions and actions, self-leadership empowers you to align your values, priorities and purpose with your daily choices and behaviours.

Your exploration of self-leadership should revolve around cultivating a deep sense of self-awareness through introspection to uncover the patterns that shape your thoughts and behaviour, revealing any limiting beliefs or assumptions that may impede your progress. By shedding light on these internal dynamics, you can create space for personal growth and transformation.

I want you to assume the role of captain in navigating the vast sea of possibilities. With unwavering confidence and a clear sense of purpose, you can then unlock your innate leadership qualities, harness your latent talents and tap into an endless well of creativity and resilience, just as I did on my self-leadership journey. Peel back the layers of your authentic self, delve into the depths of your potential and chart a course towards extraordinary performance.

I'm sure that many of you have completed high-profile leadership and executive programmes and obtained various qualifications. But what truly differentiates you? I'm going to take you back to PRINCIPLE 1 and the concept of thinking driving your emotions and behaviour. Therefore, to lead successfully you must be able to manage your thinking, your feelings and your behaviour. Understand yourself and take your leadership to the next level.

What is self-leadership?

Self-leadership is often described as the ability to influence and direct your thoughts and actions to successfully reach goals and build a satisfying life. You may consult with others for outside perspectives and opinions but ultimately you make your own decisions, motivate yourself to act and reward yourself for success.

The most important story that you can tell is the one that you tell yourself, because it will have a significant influence on your confidence as a leader. Your internal thoughts, beliefs and perceptions are without a doubt the single biggest influence in all areas of your life. Your mind is running wild with non-stop commentary and feedback on whatever's happening in your daily life. You may not always be conscious of it but this self-talk runs continually in the background. What you're saying to yourself has a huge impact on how you think, which influences your attitudes, which in turn determines your actions. Self-leadership requires you to acknowledge, understand and change that self-talk to consistently create healthy, productive actions.

Self-leadership is the practice of setting the course for your own life and finding the motivation to succeed. The concept of self-leadership first emerged in a 1983 text on organisational management by Charles C Manz in which he explained that self-leadership involves directing yourself towards tasks you're naturally motivated to complete and managing yourself to complete necessary work when you don't have motivation. Today, self-leading is widely recognised as the facilitation of behaviours that produce good mentors and team leaders as well as an overall practice of personal wellbeing and positive psychology.

The development of self-leadership skills is pivotal to becoming an effective leader because it enhances your self-awareness and self-management capabilities. In many ways self-leadership is underpinned by self-awareness and the ability to discern how your own emotions or personal biases may affect your decision making. When you can recognise your own competencies and challenges, you can set out a clearer path towards your leadership goals.

I often meet high-performance leaders who tend to be highly critical of themselves. If you recognise this in yourself, I can promise you that through self-awareness you'll discover that this self-criticism stems from fear of failure. Acknowledge this pattern and challenge it by reframing your mindset. Embrace mistakes as opportunities for growth and replace self-criticism with self-compassion. Celebrate your successes, no matter how small, and use them as stepping stones towards achieving greater goals.

Leadership experts generally agree that self-leadership is a critical first step in becoming an effective leader because it lays the foundation for leading others. In mastering self-leadership, these are the things that a successful high-performing leader excels at.

+ **Understanding your strengths, weaknesses and values:** You become self-aware and have a clear understanding of your personal goals and aspirations. By understanding yourself, you will lead with authenticity and integrity.

+ **Understanding the importance of building self-confidence**: This is a key aspect of self-leadership that you can achieve by setting measurable goals and recognising personal achievements. Without self-confidence, you may struggle to inspire and motivate others.

+ **Possessing emotional intelligence:** This is the ability to recognise and manage your own emotions and the emotions of others and is a crucial factor in self-leadership. When you have emotional intelligence, you can build strong relationships and inspire trust.

+ **Committing to lifelong learning and continuous improvement:** Invest in your personal and professional development by seeking out new experiences, learning from mistakes and seeking feedback from others.

Observations

It's important to view self-leadership as your leadership core and start your leadership journey from there. In the same way that your running coach will advise you that improving your endurance is not about doing longer runs but about developing your core, I believe that self-leadership is critical to your future development and growth, especially at this stage of your career.

I often describe self-leadership as the art of taking responsibility for your own personal and professional development. It's about cultivating the mindset, behaviours and habits that drive high performance. When you become the leader of yourself, you become the master of your destiny. What's even more important is that self-leadership isn't just about managing your time or setting goals. I see it as a holistic approach that encompasses self-awareness, self-motivation, self-discipline and self-care. It's about aligning your thoughts, emotions and actions with your purpose and values and consistently making choices that support your growth.

For you, self-leadership represents the pinnacle of personal mastery, where you harness your inner strength, purpose and accountability to achieve greatness. It's your conscious choice to rise above mediocrity, take control of your actions and constantly strive for growth and improvement. High-performance leaders like you understand that self-leadership is the catalyst that propels them to new heights of success.

I vividly recall standing on the 23rd floor of the United Nations Campus in Bonn during a coffee break at a leadership training event and overhearing a participant talking about a peer of hers, John, also a coaching client of mine. It transpired that he had taken up a new role in central Africa but previously had been her manager in the eastern Mediterranean region. I asked her to continue her story about John's self-leadership and how his leadership style stands out because he leads by example, and she obliged.

She said, 'He doesn't just talk about self-leadership; he lives it through relentless action. John is someone who continually seeks to expand his knowledge, enhance his skills and challenge the status quo. He never settles for past achievements and consistently pushes his own boundaries. Through his embodiment of self-leadership, John creates a culture of innovation, accountability and continuous improvement in his organisation. His passion for progress permeates throughout the company, inspiring team members to think creatively, take ownership of their work and fearlessly experiment. He encourages calculated risks, views failures as opportunities for growth and celebrates collective achievements. As a coach, I know how remarkable the impact of John's self-leadership is. Under his guidance, I saw his agency experience unprecedented impact. Teams thrive, individuals flourish and they are clearly also motivated to share their experiences with others.'

By now I'm sure that you appreciate the power of self-leadership and how your success will largely be determined by your ability to develop advanced self-leadership skills that enable you to better navigate complex situations. When you're a high-performing leader, you're on top of the self-leadership game. Here are the standout traits I've observed on a regular basis.

Observation #1: They make self-care a top priority

If you've never given much thought to the importance of self-care, now's the time to start. It's such an important part of your leadership development and something that some of the world's most successful leaders have made a top priority. I recall seeing Mary Barra, the CEO of General Motors, speak publicly about her approach to leadership and self-care, emphasising the importance of mindfulness, exercise and spending time with family and friends to maintain her wellbeing.

Your leadership success journey is about maintaining a consistently high performance and the secret to that lies in your self-care. Yet leaders often overlook their wellbeing, especially during times of high stress. You can't expect to help others if you haven't first helped yourself. Being a great leader means first taking care of yourself.

If you're simply waiting for some spare time to materialise in your busy schedule for self-care, it will not happen. I expect you to be proactive in making time. Prioritising self-care doesn't mean setting aside huge chunks of time in your day. Neither is it about going on retreat for a week.

Focusing on your self-care requires you to set aside as little as five, ten or 15 minutes. For example, in five minutes, you can listen to your favourite piece of music, do a short breathing exercise, get up from your desk and make yourself a drink. In 15 minutes you can declutter your workspace, write a list of goals for the week, take a power nap or just sit and meditate. In 30 minutes you can meet a friend or go for a walk.

The science behind it is compelling. When you exercise, your body releases chemicals called endorphins that trigger a positive feeling in the body. Listening to music triggers a release of dopamine, another naturally occurring happy hormone in the brain. Being out in the fresh air increases your levels of serotonin, a neurotransmitter that can improve your mood. Taking a mental break, using other parts of your brain and integrating something you truly enjoy doing two or three times a day contribute a huge amount to your self-care. As an entrepreneur and working parent, I'm a great fan of a proactive approach to self-care. Now, if you're thinking 'This is all well and good but I don't have the time', I say make time for it. Do you have a self-care routine? Do you keep to it?

While I'm not a fan of a prescriptive approach to self-care, I'd like to share a few ideas with you so you can start considering one or review your existing routine. Regardless of your routine, the mantra I keep saying to clients and to myself is this: design a routine that works for you, iterate and experiment first but keep to it. It's the same with books: best when read versus purchased and put on the shelf.

The good news is that you don't have to do it alone. My husband is a corporate executive, and for him self-care is not a luxury but a priority. While he starts every workday with a 20-minute fitness workout, I embrace the power of a 20-minute meditation and finish with my gratitude journal. Every day I write down three things that I'm grateful for. And gratitude is an attitude that has far-reaching benefits. By this time, I've sipped a glass of lemon water slowly and mindfully, and when my husband arrives with my favourite cup of coffee in bed before starting my day, I have another reason to express my gratitude.

A critical aspect of self-care that's not as frequently spoken about is setting healthy boundaries. It involves defining and communicating your limits, both to yourself and to others, in order to protect your time, energy and wellbeing. By establishing and upholding boundaries, you create a foundation for self-respect, self-care and overall effectiveness as a leader. Defining your limits can help you manage stress, take care of your physical wellbeing and create healthier relationships in both your professional and personal life.

You need boundaries to develop autonomy, improve decision making and communicate effectively but also to avoid burnout. Boundaries enable you to practise self-care and self-respect and most importantly separate your needs, thoughts and feelings and desires from those of others. It's vital to know your limits so you can set your boundaries at work and be direct in stating your boundaries to avoid confusion.

This may mean that you decide to set boundaries around your availability by designating specific hours for uninterrupted work and blocking off time for meetings and collaboration. Nobody is a mind reader, so don't forget to clearly communicate these boundaries so you can reduce interruptions, increase productivity and create a healthy work–life integration.

Be mindful that establishing boundaries around your workload and responsibilities is essential to prevent burnout and maintain a sustainable level of performance. Learn to say 'no' when necessary and delegate tasks appropriately. Recognise your limitations and set realistic expectations for yourself and others. If you're uncomfortable with a hard 'no', try 'not yet' or 'not now' instead. For example, you might set boundaries by delegating tasks that are outside your expertise or workload capacity to others who are better suited for them. By doing so, you ensure that you can focus on your core responsibilities while empowering others to contribute their skills and expertise.

With the rise of accessibility and ease of communication via various platforms and social media channels, it's more important than ever to set boundaries that protect your personal time, self-care activities and the space needed for reflection and recharging. Establish healthy habits such as exercise, meditation or hobbies and ensure they're non-negotiable parts of your routine. It doesn't have to take up hours or involve a huge amount of resources. You may set boundaries by allocating time each day for exercise or by implementing a technology-free hour before bed to promote better sleep. By honouring these boundaries, you'll enhance your overall wellbeing, resilience and ability to lead effectively.

Before moving forward, I want you to list the boundaries that are important for you and write down how you will ensure that you keep to them.

Observation #2: They manage their energy

Leaders who are able to harness and direct energy effectively tend to have high emotional intelligence. They can recognise and manage their own emotions as well as the emotions of others, which enables them to build strong relationships and foster a positive culture.

Welcome to an exploration of a vital yet often overlooked aspect of your journey to success: energy management. Energy is the life force that fuels your thoughts, emotions and actions. It's one of the foundations upon which your leadership abilities are built. Managing your energy is not simply about time management but also about optimising the quality, focus and vitality you bring to your leadership. When you strategically harness and replenish your energy, you ignite a profound transformation within yourself and your team.

Most people who encounter me might label me an extrovert, noting the abundant energy I exude during training sessions or public speaking events. Yet once these engagements conclude, I rarely mingle. Instead, I retreat into activities such as reading, meditating or playing drums that replenish my energy in a decidedly non-social way. The reality? I'm not an extrovert but an outgoing introvert. While I can thrive in social environments, I also deeply cherish my solitary moments.

The terms 'outgoing introvert' and 'reserved extrovert' might initially seem contradictory; therefore it's crucial to understand that 'reserved' and 'introvert' are not interchangeable terms and neither are 'outgoing' and 'extrovert'. An outgoing person can be either introverted or extroverted and, similarly, a reserved individual could identify with either side. The labels 'reserved' and 'outgoing' indicate your preferred mode of engagement and communication (please refer to PRINCIPLE 7 and the DISC model for a deeper understanding of this). In contrast, 'introverted' and 'extroverted' relate to how you draw and replenish energy.

So do you consider yourself more introverted or extroverted? Here's a quick way to assess it. Imagine you have four uninterrupted hours. Would you opt for a quiet solo activity or prefer to spend that time socialising with friends? Your answer will help determine whether you or your team members lean more towards introversion or extroversion. Regardless of the results, remember that as a hard-working leader, you can't afford to overlook the importance of managing your energy. Mastering this art is the key to unlocking unparalleled leadership success.

As the award-winning life coach Simon Alexander Ong says in his book *Energize* (2022), energy is everything. It's the fuel that drives your success and gives you the power to achieve your potential. And when managed well, it will transform the way you live and work. While there are plenty of other useful tips available on this topic, I encourage you to read Simon's book.

As a senior leader, you carry immense responsibility, juggling multiple priorities and navigating complex challenges. Amid this demanding landscape, managing your energy becomes crucial for sustaining peak performance, maintaining wellbeing and inspiring your team. I want you to start by reflecting on this topic. If you're like many of my clients, you probably don't pay much attention to your energy until it's running low. Let's change this together. I'd like to share some practical yet impactful strategies that you and your team can try out.

Energy audit: Conduct regular energy audits to identify activities or environments that drain or invigorate you. Reflect on which tasks or interactions leave you feeling energised or depleted. Delegate or minimise energy-draining activities and seek opportunities to engage in tasks that align with your strengths and passions.

Self-care rituals: Prioritise self-care activities that nourish your body, mind and soul. Engage in regular exercise, practise mindfulness or meditation and cultivate hobbies or interests that bring you joy and relaxation. These rituals will replenish your energy reserves, enhance your focus and promote overall wellbeing.

Purposeful rest: Recognise the importance of rest and recovery in maintaining optimal energy levels. Incorporate breaks into your schedule, take short walks or practise deep breathing exercises. Give yourself permission to step away from work and recharge, allowing for renewed focus and creativity.

Foster meaningful connections: Nurture relationships that energise and inspire you. Engage in purposeful networking, attend industry events or participate in leadership forums to connect with like-minded professionals who challenge and uplift you. Seek out mentorship or coaching relationships that provide guidance and support.

Observation #3: They stay in the present

Your ability to fully engage with the here and now is not only a cornerstone of personal fulfilment but also a vital skill for achieving consistently high performance as a leader. By cultivating present-moment awareness, you can enhance your self-leadership capabilities, unlock your full potential and inspire those around you. Are you ready to embark on this transformative journey? Then let's start with embracing the power of perspective.

The past is hindsight, the future is foresight but insight comes from the present. As a coach I'd say that past experiences live in the past, stress lives in the future and you as a leader live in the present. A vitally important part of effective leadership is to spend more time being mindful and in the present.

It's easy to look back and say 'I used to be like this, or I used to do this or that', but that's all in the past. There's nothing wrong with reflecting on past experiences but dwelling on them for too long is a sure sign that you're living in the past most of the time. Similarly, focusing on the future and the anxiety that comes from thinking 'What if this, what if that' means you're not living in the present and therefore you're not in the same place as everyone else in the room. No one spends all their time in the present but leaders who are acutely aware of this and spend most of their time in the present are the leaders who perform consistently at a high level.

That vicious cycle of 'what if, what if, what if' also triggers meta-emotions, meaning the way that we feel about our feelings. For example, let's say you've delivered a terrible board presentation. There were a lot of questions you should've been able to answer but couldn't. It wasn't your finest moment. That's a fact and it's now in the past. But you agonise over it and often what manifests itself is the meta-emotion of guilt. Now you feel guilty and think that, with your experience, you should've been able to handle things better. This feeling starts circling, occupying your thoughts, distracting you from other responsibilities and then you're stuck. How are you going to break that cycle and move forward? You need to acknowledge that it wasn't a good presentation, stay in the present, move on and decide how you'll avoid a similar situation.

I'm sure you're familiar with the examples I've just shared. In the dynamic and rapidly evolving business environment, it's easy to get caught up in the whirlwind of tasks, deadlines and future-oriented thinking. However, true self-leadership requires a conscious effort to anchor yourself in the present moment. The present is where we have the most influence and the greatest potential to make a positive impact. When you're fully present, you tap into your inner resources, make better decisions and connect more deeply with others.

One question that might be occupying your mind right now is 'What strategies can I use to stay in the present?' Refer back to the circles of control that we explored in PRINCIPLE 4 and ask yourself 'What am I in control of? What can I influence?' Spending too much time in the future or the past suggests that you're in the concerned zone, so be aware of that. More importantly, take action. Think about what you're going to do next and then choose the smallest activity to help you break that cycle of regret over past events and anxiety about future situations. This will help you refocus on the present.

Another highly effective strategy is mindfulness meditation, a powerful tool for training your mind to stay present. Begin by finding a quiet space to sit comfortably and uninterrupted for a few minutes. Close your eyes, bring your attention to your breath and observe each inhalation and exhalation without judgement. As thoughts arise, gently acknowledge them and bring your focus back to your breath. By consistently practising mindfulness meditation, even for just a few minutes each day, you'll develop greater focus, clarity and awareness. This enhanced state of presence will positively impact your decision making, problem solving and overall effectiveness as a leader.

Active listening is a key component of present-moment leadership. When conversing with colleagues, team members or clients, make a conscious effort to be fully present and attentive. Set aside any preconceived notions, judgements or distractions and focus on truly understanding the other person. Listen with curiosity, ask open-ended questions and provide meaningful feedback. By actively listening, you not only strengthen your relationships but also gain valuable insights and make better-informed decisions.

I want to close the loop on staying in the present by sharing a practical example. I first met Amina in her previous role but now she's the team leader in a fast-paced advertising agency and is responsible for managing multiple client projects simultaneously. She recognised that staying present is crucial for maintaining focus, leading effectively and meeting deadlines and asked me if I could help her and her team. Here are the five strategies she and her team used and that you can also try out.

Single-tasking: Instead of constantly switching between tasks, Amina and her team committed to single-tasking. For example, when reviewing a client's marketing campaign, they dedicated their full attention to analysing the content, design and strategy without being distracted by other pending projects.

Time blocking: Amina allocated specific time blocks for different activities and adhered to them. During these blocks, she avoids interruptions and distractions, allowing herself to fully engage with the task at hand. This way, she can focus on one project without being overwhelmed by the multitude of tasks demanding her attention.

Active presence in meetings: During team meetings or discussions, Amina actively practises being present. She made it her mission to actively listen to team members, maintain eye contact and offer her undivided attention. By doing so, she created an atmosphere of trust and engagement, encouraging open dialogue and collaboration among team members, which was vital for project success.

Mindful decision making: When faced with important decisions, Amina took a moment to pause, reflect and evaluate the available information. She considered the present circumstances, consulted relevant stakeholders and assessed potential consequences before making a well-informed choice. This approach helped her make decisions that weren't solely influenced by past experiences or future concerns but were grounded in the present reality.

Stress management techniques: Finally but crucially, she acknowledged that stress could impede the ability to stay present. Therefore she regularly practised stress management techniques such as deep breathing exercises, taking short breaks or engaging in physical activity to reduce stress levels and bring her focus back to the present moment. She has encouraged her team to follow suit.

By consciously implementing these practices, Amina demonstrated and role modelled her commitment to staying present. This didn't go unnoticed by her team and management and after our initial engagement she consistently completed her projects on a scope. This methodology has now become a blueprint for staying in the present throughout her entire organisation.

REFLECT AND GROW

Here are the three key takeaways from PRINCIPLE 6:

+ *Self-leadership is not a 'nice to have' but a must for successful, high-performing leaders because leadership starts with you and without you, there's no leadership.*
+ *Make self-care your top priority and carefully manage your energy.*
+ *Your ability to fully engage in the here and now is the cornerstone of your high-performance leadership success because insight comes from staying in the present.*

Reflect on the three points below:

+ *How will you take your and your team's self-leadership to the next level?*
+ *Choose three different strategies of self-leadership to try out in the next six months.*
+ *Who will you take on the journey with you? Remember, accountability and sharing really do help to achieve your self-leadership development goals.*

YOUR PERFORMANCE ADVANTAGE HACK

If you've never meditated, give it a go. You can use an app such as Headspace, where you can find meditation practices for busy leaders like you. You can start with as little as three minutes. Just do it regularly. Trust me, you'll feel the effects after a week. It's an excellent way to focus and quieten the mind.

PRINCIPLE 7

FOSTER THE ART OF COMMUNICATION

The art of communication is the language of leadership. –
James Humes

There's an undeniable truth about communication. The higher you go on your leadership journey, the more visible you become but, paradoxically, the less direct visibility you have. What does this actually mean and why is it relevant to you?

As a leader, you are extremely visible and the higher you go, the more you are seen and watched by everyone. Therefore how you choose to communicate is crucial. However, the higher you go, the less direct communication you'll have within your organisation, proportionate to its size. Be mindful of the fact that some staff may only see you once a year for a few minutes, or via social media, or a public announcement or speech, or a town hall meeting.

To fully grasp the significance of communication in the sphere of your leadership, it's imperative to understand that visibility and impact aren't synonymous. As you climb higher on the leadership ladder, the spotlight intensifies, illuminating your every action and decision. Ironically, your heightened visibility often comes at the cost of genuine connection and understanding. True impact isn't measured by the magnitude of your visibility but by your ability to communicate effectively and inspire those around you. Therefore, if you're serious about creating an impact as a leader, you must shift your perspective on communication to take your leadership to the next level.

I was 22 when I first consciously thought about communication. I was on a flight from Budapest to London when the reality of relocation dawned on me. I felt my heart pounding in my chest as I thought, 'How will I be able to communicate authentically while speaking a new language, going to business school and running a business in a foreign country?' It was a whole new game. Would my communication skills literally be lost in translation? That sinking feeling intensified. Was it a smart move to disadvantage myself so much when I'd achieved great success in Hungary as an entrepreneur? Why challenge myself?

What quickly became evident was that operating in English, a foreign language, didn't mean I'd lose the power of body language or my authenticity. Nor was I losing my interest in and dedication to understanding others. I ended up spending most of my adult life in the UK. It wasn't easy, especially at the beginning, but I reached one very important conclusion. Communication goes beyond words and language. It's about connecting to other human beings and taking an interest in understanding them so that you can communicate your message and thoughts in a way that they understand and is meaningful to them.

The phrase 'excellent communication skills' is one that I see and hear so often during coaching sessions and on CVs and LinkedIn profiles, but what does it mean? Specifically, what does it mean now, in your current role? And how can you maximise the power of communication to elevate your leadership success?

The effectiveness of your communication can make or break your career but it can also affect the reputation of your organisation. As a leader, maintaining your organisation's reputation is a core responsibility. This is exactly why your communication skills need to become your closest ally.

Cast your mind back to 2014, when General Motors was facing a huge crisis after it was revealed that faulty ignition switches in some of its cars had led to multiple deaths and injuries. The scandal exposed serious flaws in GM's corporate culture and sparked widespread criticism of the company's leadership.

CEO Mary Barra had only been in the role a few months. However, she quickly took action to address the issue and communicate with the public, demonstrating a willingness to take responsibility for the company's failures and a commitment to transparency and accountability. She appeared before Congress to answer tough questions about the scandal and outlined a plan for GM to prevent similar problems from occurring in the future.

Throughout the crisis, Barra communicated openly and empathetically with the public, acknowledging the seriousness of the situation and the need for change. She also made a point of listening to feedback from customers, employees and other stakeholders and incorporating their perspectives into GM's response to the crisis.

You and I both know that communicating effectively is never easy, especially in times of crisis when all eyes are on you. Her communication was widely praised for its effectiveness and authenticity. She demonstrated strong leadership skills, maintaining a clear focus on GM's values and long-term goals while also addressing the immediate crisis at hand. Her communication helped to restore trust in GM and rebuild the company's reputation in the wake of the scandal – no small task for any executive, especially if you're as new to your role as Barra was.

Elevate your communication

Communication is the cornerstone of an organisation's culture, functioning as a visible reflection of its core values, beliefs and operational procedures. The methods your organisation employs to give feedback, facilitate meetings, disseminate decisions and engage with stakeholders and staff provide critical insights into its cultural fabric.

A practical approach to understanding this dynamic involves observation. Personally, I make a point of arriving early for meetings, utilising that time to observe the reception area. Monitoring the interactions among staff members offers an immediate and informative glimpse into the organisation's culture and leadership style. This passive observation can reveal critical elements of workplace communication and interaction, thereby helping to discern the organisation's overall cultural blueprint.

It has been said that communication is the bridge between confusion and clarity.

While researching this book, I set out to discover how many books have been published globally in the past 25 years with the words 'leadership' and 'communication' in their title. According to WorldCat, the figure is more than 15,000. While other sources differ slightly, there's clearly no shortage of literature on the topic – and rightly so. Communication is fundamental to high-performance leadership. However, my goal in this chapter is not to focus on the basics of communication but rather on how to elevate your communication skills as you continue your leadership and career journey.

I want you to give some thought to the quality of your communication. What's most relevant for you? Regardless of your experience and seniority, some aspects of communication are non-negotiable:

1. **You must be able to communicate clearly**, persuasively and confidently to influence and motivate your team, build strong relationships with stakeholders and navigate challenging situations. Your messages must be easy to understand and free from jargon or technical terms that may be unfamiliar to your audience.

2. **You need to be authentic**, genuine and sincere in your communication, even when the news you're sharing isn't good. Be honest and transparent in your communication. Avoid sounding rehearsed or scripted and instead speak from the heart, because this really is the key to building trust and credibility with employees and other stakeholders.

3. **Communication is a two-way process**, so you must employ active listening when it comes to acknowledging the feedback and concerns of your

employees and stakeholders. Not only does this demonstrate your respect for the people you work with but it also helps to identify issues before they become major problems. Proactive listening, the art of focusing on the speaker, asking clarifying questions and summarising what has been said is also important, as it shows the speaker that you're engaged and interested in what they have to say. Be open to feedback and willing to make changes based on what you hear. This shows that you value other people's opinions and are committed to continual improvement.

4. **Emotional intelligence** is critical to effective communication. Be acutely aware of your emotions and how they impact the way you communicate. This also means recognising and responding to the emotions of others, which will allow you to connect on a deeper level and build stronger relationships.

5. **Think about channel diversity**. Different people prefer to receive information in different ways, so get comfortable with using a variety of communication channels, including face-to-face meetings, email, video calls and social media. Communicate regularly, even if it's only to provide updates on progress. It builds trust and keeps everyone on the same page. It goes without saying that when it comes to communication you must lead by example. This means demonstrating the same behaviour you'd expect from others and holding yourself accountable for your actions and words.

I encourage you to be mindful of the habits that lead to poor communication. I've seen this many times. For example, some executives insist on using technical jargon or vague language that their teams may not understand, creating confusion and ultimately disengagement. Some leaders are poor listeners, especially when it comes to hearing their team members' feedback or concerns, which leads to a lack of trust and engagement. Others lack empathy when they communicate, demonstrating their failure to understand the perspective of their team members, which could also hurt engagement and trust.

As a leader you'll have a preferred communication style but is it appropriate or effective for every member of the team? Probably not. Therefore you must be flexible and adapt to different communication styles to ensure that your message is received correctly. A lack of consistency is another cause of poor communication. With so many channels available, communication can easily become fragmented and diluted, creating confusion. Consistency in messaging is essential to building trust and maintaining alignment within the organisation. Failure to communicate the 'why' behind your decisions is one of the most telling signs of an ineffective communicator. When people don't understand the 'why', they become disengaged. Communicating the rationale behind your decisions will help to build trust and alignment within your organisation.

One of the best examples of effective communication that I can recall took place in 2020, when the Covid-19 pandemic had a major impact on the travel and tourism industry, with many companies facing unprecedented challenges and uncertainty. In response to the crisis Clare Gilmartin, the CEO of Trainline (a leading online European ticket retailer), communicated regularly with employees, customers and investors using a range of channels, including email updates, video messages and social media. She was transparent about the impact of the pandemic on Trainline's business and outlined specific measures that the company was taking to protect its employees and customers and to adapt to the changing market conditions.

One particularly effective example of Gilmartin's communication was a video message she recorded in March 2020, shortly after the start of the pandemic. She spoke directly to Trainline's employees, acknowledging the anxiety and uncertainty they were feeling and emphasising the importance of staying connected and supporting each other.

Her message was empathetic and inspiring and conveyed a sense of strong leadership and vision for the company's future. By communicating openly and transparently with employees and other stakeholders, she helped to build trust and confidence in Trainline during a challenging time for the travel industry. It's a benchmark of communication skills that all high-performing leaders should aspire to.

Observations

Communication is an art in itself. However, as you already know from PRINCIPLE 6, the most important story you can tell is the story you tell yourself. Your perceptions shape your interpretation of everything around you, including your colleagues and your context. I'm frequently asked what makes the biggest difference as a leader in terms of communication. I believe it's your perception and the position you take on it.

A significant proportion of communication is nonverbal. Be mindful about your body language and make sure it matches your verbal communication and energy levels. It takes less than a minute to convey authenticity. That's the time it will take your audience to make a judgement about you and decide whether or not they want to trust you. Human decision making is a combination of biases and judgements, so turn this to your advantage.

How well you communicate as a leader will be pivotal to your future success, so think about how you can improve it. What's your marginal gain in communication? A significant observation that I've made in high-performing leaders is their ability to take their political astuteness and awareness of their communication impact to a new level. For them, communication is a priority. Here are my top three observations.

Observation #1: They make their audience feel valued, understood and connected

Effective communication requires you to have a clear understanding of your audience, so take the time to understand the perspectives and needs of your employees, stakeholders and customers and tailor your communication accordingly. Be consciously aware of the implications of your communication, both verbal and nonverbal.

I'm naturally curious and over the years this has led me to connect with many amazing people. I can confirm that, for me, the phrase 'the world is a small place' is not a cliché but a reality. How have I created such a large circle of friends, colleagues and contacts? I used to think I was lucky but eventually I came to realise that my genuine interest in people and their stories drives my behaviour. It has become something of a running joke but many of the conversations that I have with clients, leaders and friends often begin with them saying 'I'm sure that you already know but...' before they share something.

Be the leader who makes people feel valued in their presence. Be the leader who listens to understand and not respond. Be the trusted leader. I recently discussed this topic with a client, a CEO whose organisation is going through a major transformation. I sought her perspective on the importance of communication during restructuring. She highlighted the importance of ensuring that everyone in the company was on the same page and understood the imminent changes. She decided to hold a town hall meeting with all employees early on in the process, even though she didn't have all the information or answers to everyone's questions.

During the meeting, she acknowledged that change can be difficult and that restructuring might create some uncertainty. She then explained the rationale behind the restructuring and what the company hoped to achieve as a result. She allocated time to answer questions from employees, addressing their concerns and providing additional context where needed, emphasising the value that the company placed on its employees and its commitment to supporting them throughout the process.

Throughout this process she maintained a calm and confident demeanour, projecting a sense of leadership and responsibility. Importantly, she used clear and concise language, avoiding jargon or technical terms that might confuse some employees. After the meeting, she followed up with an email summarising the key points discussed and provided additional resources for employees who wanted to learn more. By communicating empathetically and with authority, she was able to build trust during a challenging time for her company – no small task, as you'll know from your own experience.

Allow me to introduce you to an invaluable solution that can empower you as a leader to master the art of making your audience feel genuinely valued, deeply understood and profoundly connected. After just 15 minutes of your valuable time, DISC profiling has the potential to revolutionise your ability to establish meaningful connections, both in professional and private settings.

In an influential book titled *Emotions of Normal People* (1928), William Moulton Marston embarked on a ground-breaking exploration of observable behaviour within a specific context. His research delved into the intricate relationship between our inherent personality styles, shaped by natural inclinations and external influences. This concept highlights the dynamic interplay between our internal make-up and the external factors that shape our behaviours.

Within his book, Marston presented an extensive body of research and a comprehensive theory known as the DISC model. This model groups behavioural characteristics into four distinct divisions referred to as personality styles. Each style encompasses a set of observable behavioural traits commonly associated with individuals who share that particular style. Through this framework, Marston not only identified these four personality styles but also devised a method to gauge an individual's inclination towards exhibiting behaviours aligned with each style.

We all have different preferences or areas of focus that influence how we communicate and how we prefer to be communicated with. There are as many as 41 different combinations of DISC profiles; however, for simplicity and ease of use of the framework, I'll focus on the four key preferences and drivers to help you better understand yourself and others.

Ultimately, I recommend using the DISC model as a guide that can empower you to establish stronger connections, foster collaboration and enhance overall communication. Every coaching programme I undertake starts with DISC – a personal assessment framework that helps leaders to understand themselves and also to understand others at a pace that, in my experience, no other models can. But judge for yourself.

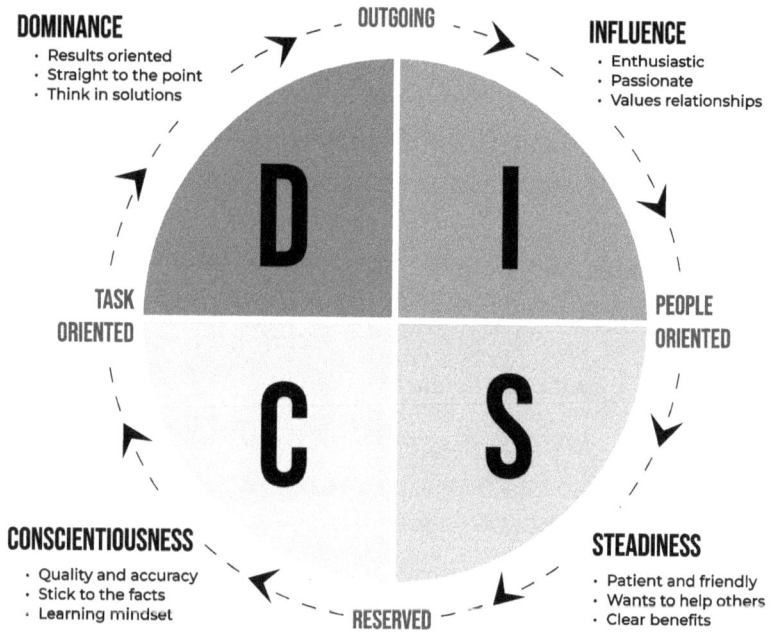

Figure 6: The DISC model

DISC personality profiles provide a powerful tool for leaders like you who are looking to enhance their connection and communication skills. The model categorises individuals into four primary personality styles: **Dominance (D), Influence (I), Steadiness (S) and Conscientiousness (C).** Each style represents a distinct pattern of behaviour, communication preferences and approaches to work and relationships.

Understanding these personality profiles can provide leaders with valuable insights into their own communication style and help them to adapt their approach to connect effectively with others. Here's a brief overview of each personality style and its implications for connection and communication:

Dominance (D):

Individuals with a dominant style are direct, assertive and results oriented. They value taking charge, making decisions and achieving goals. When connecting with dominant individuals, leaders should be concise, focused and emphasise the bottom line. Engaging them in problem-solving discussions and allowing them to take the lead can foster a sense of connection and respect.

Influence (I):

Influential individuals are outgoing, sociable and charismatic. They thrive on building relationships, inspiring others and generating enthusiasm. Leaders can connect with influential individuals by engaging in open and friendly conversations, recognising their contributions and providing opportunities for collaboration and social interaction.

Steadiness (S):

Individuals with a steady style are patient, supportive and reliable. They prioritise harmony, cooperation and stability. Leaders can establish a connection with steady individuals by showing empathy, actively listening and creating a supportive environment. Providing clear expectations, involving them in decision making and recognising their loyalty can also enhance communication and connection.

Conscientiousness (C):

Conscientious individuals are detail oriented, analytical and precise. They value accuracy, organisation and systematic approaches. To connect with conscientious individuals, leaders should provide well-researched information, be prepared and respect their need for accuracy. Allowing them time to process information, involving them in planning and recognising their expertise can encourage a feeling of connection and trust.

Where do your preferences lie? What's the personality style of your different team members or your manager? Before writing your next email, delivering your next presentation or preparing for your team performance review, consider how you could use DISC to elevate your communication to the next level.

When it comes to making your audience feel truly valued, understood and connected, never be complacent. Whether you're running a town hall meeting, making a keynote speech or leading a meeting, take every opportunity to observe and understand your audience beforehand. Get a sense of their mood, energy and body language and use these observations to strengthen your connection with them and land your message exactly as you intended.

Whenever I'm doing a speaking engagement I always spend some time beforehand sitting at the back of the audience, observing them, to get a better sense of how I'm going to connect with them. I take the audience's perspective, which is one of the most powerful things you can do. You stop being a master communicator when you become complacent about your audience.

Observation #2: They are masters of questioning

The further you travel on your leadership journey, the less information you'll receive directly and the more filtered, refined and reviewed the information is likely to be. Mastering the art of questioning and reading between the lines is a vital skill to possess.

I believe leaders don't ask enough questions and as a result they're missing the biggest trick in the communication book. The art of questioning isn't just about asking questions; it's also about asking the right types of questions in the right way to help you gather information, make better decisions and even inspire innovation or establish a culture of collaboration. It will also improve your decision making and strategic choices. If you always think the same way, you're always going to come up with the same solutions. As a master of questioning, you'll be enhancing other people's thinking and encouraging greater sharing.

It's important to differentiate between transactional questions and transformational questions. Transactional questions can be described as transactions of information between two people. People tend to ask transactional questions when they want something. On the other hand, transformational questions create a transformation in your thinking and that of the person you're communicating with. There are three types of transformational questions that you need to become familiar with: open ended, probing and reflective.

Always try to ask open-ended questions rather than closed questions that simply invite yes and no answers. Open-ended questions typically begin with a 'how', 'what' or 'why'. They are enquiry based and open up that discussion and conversation. For example, you might ask 'What are some of the challenges you and your team are currently facing?' or 'How can we improve customer experience?'

I'd also advise caution when using 'why' because certain personalities can interpret it as a criticism. So rather than asking 'Why did your team choose this project plan?', a better question would be 'What's the reason that you and your team chose this project?' as this completely refocuses the question.

Ask probing questions. These get to the detail quickly and can help to uncover underlying issues and assumptions. A good example of a probing question is 'Can you explain it in a bit more detail?' or 'What led you to this conclusion?' But it can also be about encouraging discussion and uncovering hidden or potential issues. Probing questions are important for gathering more in-depth information but also for better engagement.

Ask reflective questions. These encourage self-reflection and promote learning and growth. Sometimes you want your employees to think critically about their work and identify improvements. So you might ask 'What did you learn from this experience?', 'How could you approach this differently in the future?' or 'What skills do you need to develop?' I recommend asking questions that encourage discussion, produce information and make the people in your team more reflective. The result will be a stronger relationship and closer connections.

Observation #3: They are good story thinkers

In business, storytelling is a valuable tool for sharing compelling, relatable stories rather than just facts and figures. Stories are a powerful way of communicating and connecting with your colleagues and employees or, in fact, anyone who's connected to your organisation. However, to tell a story, you need to think in a story. I see too many leaders putting way too much emphasis on delivery and giving less attention to considering the audience, context and message.

Go back to PRINCIPLE 1: everything starts with thinking. Your thinking drives your emotions and feelings, which in turn drives your behaviour. So here, story thinking will drive your behaviour as a storyteller. In this context, forget the stories you might recall from your childhood or school years. I'm talking about a story with a purpose. If you want to use a story impactfully and effectively, then you must have a clear reason for telling it. For example, you might want to tell a story to connect at an emotional level with those team members who generally stay quiet. If that's the purpose, think of a story that evokes empathy, connection, trust and rapport. Or you might want to tell a story about a complex topic to make it more relatable, perhaps because you're speaking to an audience of non-experts. So how do you do this? The use of analogies can be a good way of demonstrating the impact of what you're saying in a way that's easy to understand and appreciate. You can also tell a story to inspire action to motivate people towards a common goal, overcome obstacles or strive for excellence.

Another reason you might tell a story is to create a shared vision of what success looks like. You want to make it tangible for your audience because not everyone has the visibility you have, nor do they have your leadership skills and experience. Storytelling also fosters a culture of learning and it can be a powerful tool for teaching and sharing knowledge and experience, not just concerning mistakes but about successes as well.

I often work with leaders who don't see themselves as good storytellers or say 'I don't tell stories', but that doesn't matter. What matters is being a story thinker. If you're not thinking in a story, you're not going to tell an impactful story.

About five years ago I had a phone call from a former executive coaching client who worked in the global telecoms industry. He'd launched a tech start-up and needed to talk. Spencer explained that he wanted to inspire his employees and create a sense of purpose and motivation. His vision was to incorporate story thinking and storytelling into his communication style because he'd seen the impact it had created in his previous role. So we embarked on a six-month project together, establishing five key areas of intervention. It worked brilliantly, so I'd like to share it with you and encourage you to give it a go.

1. **Setting the stage:** Begin by sharing a personal story about your own journey as an entrepreneur. Describe the challenges you've faced, the failures you've experienced and the lessons you've learned along the way. By being vulnerable and sharing your story, you can create an emotional connection with your team and establish yourself as relatable and human.

2. **Painting the vision:** Create a compelling vision to inspire your team. Conjure up a vivid picture of the future, describe how your products or services will positively impact people's lives, then weave this vision into a story, highlighting the problems they're solving and the transformative outcomes they seek to achieve.

3. **Personalising the story:** Encourage your team to share their stories and experiences. After all, everyone has unique perspectives and insights that can contribute to the collective success of the organisation. By creating a safe and inclusive environment where people feel comfortable sharing their stories, you'll foster a sense of belonging and empower your employees to contribute in an authentic way.

4. **Acting as a coach:** Being a leader means nurturing the growth and development of your team members.

I strongly advocate holding one-on-one coaching sessions with your direct reports and listening attentively to their challenges and aspirations. Rather than giving direct instructions or solutions, use storytelling to guide them. Sharing stories of individuals who overcame similar obstacles and achieved success is another way of inspiring the people around you.

5. **Celebrating successes:** Motivate your team by showcasing group achievements and individual successes through storytelling. Whether it's a major product launch or an employee's personal accomplishment, highlight the journey, the obstacles that they've overcome and the lessons learned.

The value of storytelling is that it performs many functions simultaneously. It builds trust, communicates values and vision, fosters collaboration and encourages creativity. I don't know any other communication technique that's quite as impactful and effective as storytelling. Ultimately, whoever tells the best story wins.

REFLECT AND GROW

Here are the top three key takeaways from PRINCIPLE 7:

+ *The higher you go on your leadership journey, the more visible you become but paradoxically, the less direct visibility you possess.*

+ *Communication is about connection. Be conscious and deliberate. Effective communication is not a coincidence; use the DISC framework to create a competitive advantage.*

+ *Focus on your ability to ask questions and think in terms of a story.*

Reflect on the three points below:

+ *How would you describe your communication style?*

+ *Choose three different strategies for integrating storytelling that you can try out in the next six months.*

+ *If you can, ask a licensed professional to administer DISC profiles for yourself and your team. I promise it will be a game changer. However, I don't recommend the free version of online DISC profiles for this purpose.*

YOUR PERFORMANCE ADVANTAGE HACK

Take five minutes to think of three individuals whom you consider to be effective communicators. Note their traits and characteristics. What makes them successful in the art of communication? How does it impact their leadership success?

PRINCIPLE (8)

UNLEASH THE POWER OF UNLEARNING

Half of wisdom is learning what to unlearn. – Larry Niven

Are you prepared to unlearn? You may think that's a strange question because, after all, the reason you're reading this book is to learn. As former Facebook COO Sheryl Sandberg said, 'The ability to learn is the most important quality a leader can have.' However, if you want to elevate your ability to learn, you must focus on unlearning. If you don't unlearn, you risk becoming outdated and irrelevant and ultimately you'll be holding yourself and your organisation back. This is precisely why I want you to tap into the power of unlearning and consider it an important competitive advantage for your leadership success.

You may have figured out by now that I'm a passionate lifelong learner and immensely curious. However, over the past three decades as an entrepreneur and coach, I've done a lot of unlearning. I still love learning new things but unlearning at this stage of my career is just as important as it was 30 years ago. And having run countless programmes on the power of unlearning, I can tell you that it's not as easy as simply sticking an 'un' in front of the word learning.

At times it feels as though I've been in an 'unlearning boot camp' since I had my stroke, which left me partially sighted. However, the biggest unlearning of my professional life is what you're reading right now. One question I've been asked many times over the years is 'When will you be writing a book?' I stuck to my rigid belief that the work I was doing didn't lend itself to a book. The leaders, teams and organisations I worked with were all diverse and spread geographically around the world and, as a result, my approach and programmes were bespoke. How could I possibly condense all that information, put it in a book and tell you this is how you should be doing things? I also believed – again, wrongly – that it could look as if I was on an ego trip.

For years the idea of writing a book made no sense to me. But I was completely overlooking the fact that there are many reasons for writing one. People were interested because they didn't all have access to my coaching or training sessions but wanted to learn more about the philosophy and methodology I offer to senior leaders, high-performing individuals, their teams and organisations. I realised that writing a book would allow me to inspire and make even more leaders think differently, and it would act as a valuable tool. So I had to unlearn. I had to let go of a strong belief that was holding me back from being able to take all those observations and insights gained over the years and share them with other people and allow them to learn from them. That included sharing my life journey, which I never thought I'd do, but which I now see makes the book more meaningful and personal. I sincerely hope that you're on the same page as me when it comes to embracing the idea of letting go and unlearning.

Back in the 1930s, when Albert Einstein was teaching at the Institute for Advanced Study in Princeton, it was time to set the examinations for the graduating class. When Einstein handed over the exam papers to his teaching assistant, the assistant noted that it was the same paper that Einstein had set for that class the year before. The assistant asked, 'Isn't this the same exam you gave this class last year?' 'Yes, it is,' replied Einstein. Puzzled, the assistant asked, 'But how can you give the same exam to this class two years in a row?' 'Because,' replied Einstein, 'the answers have changed.'

On reflection, the fundamental questions we've been asking leaders for many years haven't changed but the answers and context have changed significantly. Just think about how the Covid-19 pandemic has impacted the world and the way we work.

According to Barry O'Reilly, author of the bestselling book *Unlearn* (2018), 'Unlearning is the process of letting go, reframing and moving away from once useful mindsets and acquired behaviours that were effective in the past but now limit our success. It is not forgetting, removing or discarding knowledge or experience; it is the conscious act of letting go of outdated information and actively engaging in taking in new information to inform effective decision making and action.'

His inspiration for writing the book came from observing leaders of Fortune 500 companies. He was fascinated to observe how they all excelled at learning new things but what they all struggled with was unlearning the past, especially if they were things that had made them successful. This is perhaps your moment to reflect before you embrace the power of unlearning and let go of what no longer serves you. As I often highlight in my keynotes, leadership requires the willingness to unlearn, re-evaluate long-held beliefs and adapt to an ever-changing world. Only by shedding old ways of thinking can we pave the way for new perspectives and possibilities.

What is unlearning?

Unlearning is not about forgetting but knowing what's relevant about what you know that you need to take to the next phase of your journey. It's also about challenging those beliefs and assumptions that are no longer serving you. Unlearning allows you to create a new perspective and use it as a competitive advantage. Many leaders will consciously learn and continue adding more courses to their repertoire but on returning to their office nothing changes. They do exactly the same things as they did before. Why? Because despite having the intention to implement the new frameworks and strategies they've learned, they haven't identified what they need to unlearn to do things differently.

Your leadership success relies heavily on constant learning, growth and evolution. However, without focus and commitment it's all too easy to become stuck in your old ways, habits and beliefs, which become barriers to your ability to innovate, adapt and lead effectively. This is where unlearning comes in – letting go of old ideas, beliefs and habits to make room for new ones.

A reluctance or refusal to unlearn can result in missed opportunities and a decline in creativity and innovation within teams and organisations. In today's rapidly changing business environment, your ability to adapt and learn quickly is critical to your success. Unlearning is not about forgetting everything you know or abandoning your values but rather about examining your assumptions and biases, challenging your beliefs and being open to new perspectives.

Unlearning can also lead to increased self-awareness, empathy and better decision making. By examining your own biases and assumptions, you become more aware of how they may be impacting your leadership style and decision-making processes. A heightened self-awareness will help you in making more informed and objective decisions, and give you a more empathetic understanding of others' perspectives.

How do you unlearn?

Unlearning isn't easy. It requires conscious effort to let go of deeply ingrained beliefs and habits and you may face many challenges in doing so. Cognitive dissonance is a mental conflict that occurs when your beliefs don't line up with your actions. You experience cognitive dissonance when you're presented with information that conflicts with your beliefs. This can be uncomfortable and may cause you to resist the new information. Confirmation bias is the tendency to interpret new evidence as confirmation of your existing beliefs or theories and ignore information that challenges them. This can make it difficult to unlearn. Then there's fear of the unknown. Stepping outside your comfort zone to try new things can be scary and create resistance to change.

One way to challenge your assumptions is to ask questions and seek out new perspectives. Engage with people who have different backgrounds, experiences and ideas. This can help you to broaden your viewpoint and see things in a new light.

All too often I see leaders who believe that micromanaging their team is the best way to ensure quality and productivity. However, as the team grows, they realise that their micromanagement stifles creativity and hinders individual growth. At this point I often recommend unlearning the belief that control equals success. By relinquishing control, empowering team members and trusting their abilities, you can foster a collaborative environment that increases productivity and innovation.

It may seem counterintuitive but failure can be an excellent opportunity for learning and growth. Instead of viewing failure as a negative experience, embrace it as a chance to unlearn old habits and beliefs. Analyse what went wrong and examine what you could've done differently. This can help you to identify areas where you may need to unlearn old habits and beliefs and develop new skills or approaches.

Self-reflection – taking time to reflect on your actions, decisions and thought processes – is a critical part of unlearning. It's important to ask yourself questions such as 'What biases or assumptions might be impacting my decision making?' or 'What beliefs do I need to let go of to be more effective as a leader?' This can help you to identify areas where you may need to unlearn old habits and beliefs.

Unlearning is key to effective leadership development. Leaders who are willing to let go of old habits and beliefs and embrace new perspectives and approaches are more likely to succeed. By challenging assumptions, learning from failure, embracing discomfort and practising self-reflection, you can continue to grow and evolve as an effective and adaptable leader.

Observations

By embracing the paradox of unlearning, recognising the need for change and cultivating a mindset of curiosity, you'll take a significant step towards becoming an even more effective leader. Remember, unlearning is not a one-time event but an ongoing journey towards growth and adaptation. It's a continuous process of letting go of old beliefs and opening up to new possibilities. At the end of my coaching and training courses, I ask one important question: what will you unlearn? And I consistently observe the same traits and characteristics in leaders who understand the importance of taking unlearning to the next level. These are my top three observations.

Observation #1: They know when to unlearn

It can be quite unsettling to realise that the things that made you successful in the past may well be the things that are stopping you from succeeding now. To recognise when unlearning might be required, high-performing leaders ask these two questions:

+ In which area do I not perform according to expectations?
+ In which area do I not create the impact I aimed for?

In my experience, people don't spend enough time unlearning. However, there's no point in learning about unlearning and then not doing it, because you're never going to change your behaviour. There is a huge assumption that people know how to unlearn, that it will somehow happen automatically. You're an experienced leader; you've learned a great deal and you'll learn a lot more. But if you don't start refocusing on the unlearning, it will limit your growth and learning capacity at this stage of your career.

Let me give you a practical example of how unlearning can positively impact your leadership development. Imagine that your organisation has embarked on a digital or cultural transformation. It's a major project and you think everything's going really well. From the feedback you've been getting the team seems happy and everyone is motivated. And you genuinely believe this. Then you come to a key progress review stage of the project and discover that the reality is completely different. Things aren't going as well as you believed. We're not talking about small mistakes that have been made or that you were unaware of; we're talking about the conflict that arises from an expectation gap that exists between you and the rest of the team. Then you start to question yourself. What caused that expectation gap? Why did I believe that people were motivated when they were clearly telling me they weren't? How did I make that judgement?

Then you need to examine your own belief system – for example, did you base your expectations on the fact that no one actually said they didn't feel motivated? Why were people not giving genuine feedback or speaking up about potential issues? Did you understand the context of the situation?

This isn't a question of your ability to run a large project, nor is it a question of people feeling unable to be motivated in a project that you're leading. But it is a situation that should prompt you to look at some of your learned habits that have perhaps worked so well so far but aren't working in this context and unlearn them.

There are other factors to consider. For example, you may have been leading a team of 20. Now you're in a new role with new responsibilities and you're leading a team of 300 in a large organisation, perhaps in a different sector. The context is different with a smaller team, not least because you'd have more one-to-one engagement and therefore better feedback. Leading the project successfully with 300 is a very different proposition, as I'm sure you'll agree.

Observation #2: They see mistakes as opportunities

I've had the privilege of witnessing, almost on a daily basis, how high-performing leaders from all corners of the globe navigate the treacherous waters of mistakes and failures. It's an undeniable truth that mistakes happen; they're an intrinsic part of the journey. But what sets these exceptional leaders apart is their unwavering belief that mistakes are not stumbling blocks but stepping stones towards greatness. They view every misstep as an opportunity, propelling their leadership competencies to new heights.

Experience has a way of sharpening your senses and elevating your understanding of the immense responsibility you have as a leader. You possess the agency to make critical decisions that shape the course of your organisations and the lives of those you lead. What's fascinating is that people often rally behind your decisions, not because they believe you're infallible but because of the weight of the role. It's a testament to the trust and respect you earned through your journey.

But here's the secret that these high-performing leaders have discovered: true power lies in how you respond when those decisions go wrong. It's easy to succumb to self-doubt or retreat into a defensive shell but the leaders who soar above the rest do something remarkable – they embrace their mistakes as golden opportunities for growth. This why I want you to recognise that failure is not a label but a launching pad to new levels of excellence. It's an opportunity for transparency and some vulnerability.

Instead of shrinking away from your missteps, stand tall, armed with an insatiable hunger for knowledge and a willingness to adapt. Analyse the situation with an observant eye, mining the underlying lessons within. In doing so you'll unlearn old habits and beliefs that no longer serve you, clearing the path for fresh insights and innovative solutions. I like to call it a 'dance of constant evolution', a symphony of unlearning. And with each step, you'll become more resilient, more agile and more equipped to face the challenges that lie ahead.

How do you embrace your mistakes with open arms and an open mind? How do you navigate the journey of transforming them from stumbling blocks into stepping stones towards greatness? I'd like you to reflect on this before you read further.

While I'm sure you're all for a post-mortem or retrospective, I'm a great fan of a project pre-mortem, which takes place before project kick-off. At this stage, you want answers to the fundamental question, 'What would stop us from succeeding?' I want you to make proactive risk assessments of potential project failure. There will undoubtedly be technical and strategic elements involved but it's important to include thinking and beliefs which could potentially derail a project.

The pre-mortem also becomes an opportunity to explore what needs to be unlearned for this particular project. I'm involved in many cultural transformations and often see technical issues or objections arising from differing views and opinions. However, you must ask the question, 'What do we need to unlearn for this project or this transformation to be successful?' This question could be the ticket to your competitive advantage, especially in our geopolitically complex world. As a leader you must walk the talk in creating a culture of unlearning and establishing a higher level of psychological safety that allows your team and organisation to experiment and innovate without fear of failure.

Observation #3: They understand and engage in the cycle of unlearning

Unlearning is a process. You don't announce, 'That's it, I've unlearned!' Like every journey, it has different stages and paths and it's cyclical in nature. You can't expect your behaviour to change simply by observing and then doing nothing about it. You can't learn new ways of working if you're not prepared to unlearn. That's not learning, it's building. You're hanging on to your beliefs and adding to them. You need to commit to doing things differently by unlearning the way that you did something previously or unlearning a fixed but no longer relevant belief and relearning a new way.

I appreciate the challenges of these mindset shifts and processes. This is precisely why I always have a smile on my face and share it with others when I witness the unlearning process resulting in tangible outcomes. A good example of this is the story of Martina, the experienced COO of a traditional manufacturing company.

Martina recognised ahead of the competition that her industry was undergoing a significant shift towards automation and digitisation. Despite her deep knowledge and experience in traditional manufacturing, she had to unlearn her biases and embrace the potential of technology to transform the organisation. By shifting her mindset, convincing the CEO and being open to new possibilities, she successfully steered her company towards innovation and emerged as a leader in the digital era. She has even been recognised in her industry for her innovative and novel approach to leadership. As I always highlight, unlearning isn't about erasing everything you've learned; it's about developing your ability to challenge your assumptions and let go of outdated mental models.

I have been preoccupied with the concept of unlearning for many years. I find Barry O'Reilly's concept of the 'cycle of unlearning' as

137

an invaluable source of wisdom. Like any other behavioural change, the more you do it, the more automatic and habitual unlearning will become.

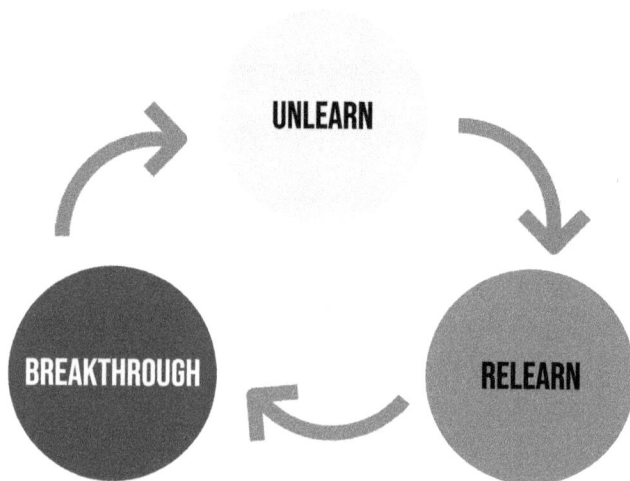

Figure 7: The cycle of unlearning (concept from O'Reilly 2018)

Step 1: Unlearn

Your first step is to recognise when and what you need to unlearn. You need to be curious and open and own the results. If you're not achieving the outcome you want, don't jump to blame somebody else. Instead, ask questions, explore, seek opinions, research, dig deeper, form hypotheses.

Step 2: Relearn

Then you need to figure out what you need to do differently. If things aren't working, think about what new behaviour might help you. If your existing behaviour(s) were working, you wouldn't need to unlearn. In this step you need to design and create a small behaviour experiment for yourself that will help you to learn. You've become a learner again and you need to get comfortable with being uncomfortable.

Step 3: Breakthrough

The final step is where you execute your behaviour experiment. See what happens when you make a small tweak or implement a small behavioural change. What did you think was going to happen? If you achieved the desired result, look to scale it up. If not, review it and try something else. Choose another behaviour or change and go through the cycle again. These small experiments are the only effective way to achieve the breakthroughs you need.

To become a high-performing leader you need to continually challenge yourself. With both technical knowledge and leadership behaviours now evolving at an unprecedented pace, unlearning will set you apart from others as you continue to develop in your role. Learning to unlearn makes way for better, more effective practices. However, it's crucial to remember that this knowledge will also change. This necessitates mental preparation for relearning. The continuous cycle of unlearning, learning and relearning can help guide you through uncharted territory. Ultimately, it comes down to your goals and objectives. To stay on course against a backdrop of disruption, uncertainty and change, unlearning and relearning are key.

Many of the challenges you'll face in effectively unlearning and relearning are created by you. First, you must be willing to adapt and be open to information that goes against your inherent beliefs, which may be at odds with what you've always been told or taught to do. Second, you may need to learn how to learn again. Finally, you must create an environment for relearning to happen in a meaningful yet often challenging space outside your existing comfort zone.

The ability to unlearn will stand you in good stead in whatever direction your leadership journey takes. It increases your adaptability; simply recognising the need to unlearn opens up the learning gap and strengthens the growth mindset that says 'I don't know everything and not everything I know is relevant to where I'm going.'

REFLECT AND GROW

Here are the top three key takeaways from PRINCIPLE 8:

+ *If you want to elevate your ability to learn, you must focus on unlearning. If you don't unlearn, you'll risk becoming outdated and irrelevant and ultimately hold yourself and your organisation back. Make learning to unlearn your leadership competitive advantage.*

+ *You need to know when to unlearn and understand and engage in the learning cycle so you can adapt fast and grow as a leader.*

+ *You must see mistakes and failures as learning opportunities.*

Reflect on the three points below:

+ *What have you unlearned and learned so far while reading this book?*

+ *Identify one key limiting belief that stops you or your team from reaching the full potential.*

+ *How do you deal with mistakes and failures? On a scale of 1 to 10, mark your answer, with 10 seeing them as significant opportunities and 1 perceiving them as obstacles. (I rate my response as a perfect 10!)*

YOUR PERFORMANCE ADVANTAGE HACK

Take five minutes to consider what you'd like to unlearn. What would make the biggest impact on your leadership success? Find your marginal gain in unlearning.

PART 3

NEXT LEVEL CAREER

PRINCIPLE 9

ELEVATE YOUR CAREER

You miss 100 per cent of the shots you don't take.
– Wayne Gretzky

When contemplating your next career move, you need to adopt a strategic mindset. Whether that entails transitioning to a new organisation or assuming a different role within your current one, careful consideration is necessary. It's essential to recognise the distinction between a job and a career, adhering to the notion that 'the job belongs to your organisation but your career belongs to you'. I want you to stop and reflect on this before you read further because this shift in perspective is truly a game changer and has proved to be a transformative catalyst to many leaders around the world with whom I've worked.

Now you understand that your chosen career trajectory is entirely in your hands, ensure that each role serves as a milestone along the way. Rather than allowing roles to dictate your aspirations, it's imperative to let your career vision guide your professional ambitions.

My WhatsApp profile says, 'The best way to predict the future is to create it.' I truly believe this quote and encourage you to think the same way about your career. Don't limit yourself by what others may or may not have done with a similar background. Follow your vision. Be true to your purpose and the magic will happen. I'm not talking about what my clients and I call a 'ballerina scenario' but a career phase that builds on your expertise and experience but most importantly you feel is fulfilling and can create an impact.

The term ballerina scenario became my codename for unrealistic options or wishful thinking, and it originated in a talk that I gave many years ago at a large corporate strategic event. While on stage I commented on something having an extremely low probability and compared it to the likelihood of me becoming a ballerina at the Royal Ballet (even though I did take ballet lessons as a child).

I might be one of the few people who actually took career advice at school. Being a high-performing student, my session with the career advisor was short and she got straight to the point, saying, 'Agnes, with these grades, you can be a doctor or a lawyer or anything you want to be.' So I took option number three and became what I wanted to be – an entrepreneur – and have been on this career path for the past 30 years since founding my first business.

I know from experience that many leaders who have worked hard for many years to reach the upper tiers of management will find those high-level roles elusive. There are no obvious reasons why this is so; these leaders are intelligent, skilled and charismatic, yet only a handful will ever reach the pinnacle. However, to borrow from the title of executive coach Marshall Goldsmith's 2008 book on climbing the last few rungs of the ladder, 'what got you here won't get you there'. And this should be your most important unlearning so far.

As a coach, I'm asked many questions about careers and job roles, from how to move to the next level internally to how to make a next-level external move. People wonder whether they can switch industries after so many years of experience and still achieve success. My answer remains that there's no reason to limit yourself. Not only can you switch industry but also sector or operational function or go from private to public and vice versa.

To subtract complexity, I have two types of career conversations with leaders. If you're reading this book you're highly likely to fall into these categories: you're either preparing and ready for your next move, or you've just landed a new role and are looking to make your mark in the first 100 days.

If you're on a mission to enter the next phase of your career and have always been headhunted for your roles, you may be unclear about what strategy you need to pursue to advance to that next phase. For many of you, this will no doubt be a big concern but my advice is that you can't play chess by following the rules of tennis. You need to understand the change in context, think differently about your next career phase, adapt and make the necessary changes quickly before you miss the opportunity.

How will what you've read so far influence the way you approach your job and most importantly your career? What will you do differently? Are you ready to think strategically about your next move?

You've achieved so much in your career so far. You've worked hard, developed your skills and climbed the ladder to success. Yet your journey is far from over and you must stay focused on the future. Your next career move could be the most thrilling and fulfilling yet but you need to think about it strategically. This involves anticipating changes, analysing trends and making informed decisions. It's time to shift gear and change your approach if necessary because as Mahatma Gandhi supposedly said, 'The future depends on what you do today.'

Designing your career strategy

Gone are the days when simply excelling in your job could guarantee a promotion. As you climb the ladder to more senior positions, a new mindset must take centre stage: strategic thinking. Why is it so crucial for leaders at this level? Allow me to explain. When you embrace strategic thinking, you unlock a whole new level of insight that empowers you to spot opportunities amid the chaos and identify potential risks lurking in the shadows. No longer confined by the limitations of the present, you develop a remarkable ability to envision the bigger picture. This foresight becomes your superpower, allowing you to anticipate changes and giving you the agility to pivot with finesse, which you will undoubtedly need in today's digital world. But it doesn't stop there. Strategic thinking should be the driving force behind your leadership. You can't passively wait for opportunities to come knocking. You need to become the architect of your destiny, actively seeking out new challenges and crafting your own path to success. By embracing this proactive mindset, you'll transcend the ordinary.

In a world where change is the only constant, staying relevant is the name of the game. This is where strategic thinking truly comes into its own. By staying on the pulse of industry trends and embracing change with open arms, you'll ensure that you're always one step ahead. Consequently you become the master of adaptation.

As you know, I love observing leadership behaviour, so when I heard that Sheryl Sandberg had become chief operating officer of Facebook, I knew that here was someone who actively sought out challenging roles. Before joining Facebook she had worked at Google and served as chief of staff to the US Treasury secretary. She had done a magnificent job of strategically positioning herself as a thought leader on topics such as leadership and women in the workplace, authoring the influential book *Lean In* (2013). Sandberg's deliberate career choices and focus on personal growth propelled her to top leadership positions. This example should inspire you to leverage your passions, expertise and foresight, embrace calculated risks, pursue diverse opportunities and continually evolve to achieve remarkable success in your career.

I hope that by now you can see why strategic thinking is not just a fancy concept. It's the key that unlocks a world of opportunities, propels you towards success and ensures your continued relevance. Embrace it, wield it and let it pave the way to the next phase of your career.

Planning the next phase of your career

A good place to start planning your next career move is with a detailed self-assessment, which involves reflecting on your strengths and weaknesses as well as your goals and aspirations. Start by identifying your core values, the guiding principles that underpin your decisions and actions. They are the things that matter most to you, both personally and professionally. Identifying your core values gives you greater clarity on what you want to achieve. I don't want you to simply make a list of your strengths and weaknesses. Seek feedback from colleagues, mentors and other trusted sources to gain a better understanding of your strengths and areas for improvement. You may wish to refer back to PRINCIPLE 2 and tap into your leadership superpower to propel you on your quest.

Finally, consider your long-term goals and aspirations. By taking a long-term view you can ensure that your next career move is aligned with your broader career goals. How does your next career move fit into that vision? With the importance of strategic thinking in mind, here are some practical tips for planning the next chapter of your career:

Reflect on your career journey: Before you start planning for the future, I want you to reflect on your career journey so far. Consider what you enjoy most about your current role as well as what you find most challenging. Identify any skills or knowledge gaps that you need to address to achieve your goals. By evaluating your successes and challenges and understanding what motivates you, you can use self-reflection to guide your next steps.

Define your goals: Identify what you want to achieve in the next chapter of your career. Be specific about the kind of work you want to do and the type of company you want to work for, as well as the sort of lifestyle that you desire. Setting clear goals will help you to stay focused and motivated.

Research your options: Study the job listings, talk to people in your network and attend industry events. Most importantly, be open to new ideas and opportunities that you may not have considered before.

Evaluate your skills: Identify your areas of expertise and focus on the areas that need improvement. This will help you understand which types of roles and industries are the best fit for your skills and experience.

Develop a plan: Detail the specific steps that you need to take to achieve your goals, set yourself timelines and, as always, be prepared to adjust your plan as necessary.

I always enjoy taking inspiration from outside the business world. In my view, Michelle Obama, the esteemed former first lady of the United States, was meticulous in the way that she crafted her career trajectory through a strategic approach rooted in education, public service and advocacy. By pursuing degrees from Princeton University and Harvard Law School, she positioned herself as a highly educated professional, laying a strong foundation for her future endeavours.

By conscientiously pursuing roles within prestigious firms and engaging in public service initiatives, she honed her skills, expanded her knowledge and developed a deep understanding of the complexities within these domains. This deliberate pursuit of professional experiences paved the way for her to later transition into the domain of non-profit work.

Driven by a strategic mindset, Michelle Obama emerged as a powerful advocate for various causes that resonated with her core values. Her relentless dedication to education, health and women's empowerment transformed her into a beacon of inspiration and influence. Through her strategic approach to career choices, she not only exemplifies the power of education and public service but serves as a role model of a leader who carved out a purposeful and influential career path.

Don't make the next phase of your career an accidental success. Take charge, engage your career game changers and set yourself up for success. Remember, strategic thinking is all about looking ahead, being proactive and staying relevant. By adopting the same principles, you can achieve your goals and continue to progress in your career.

Observations

As a successful leader, you have a wealth of experience to draw upon. However, as you approach the next phase of your career, you need to consider how you'll continue to evolve and grow. In looking to the future, you may be wondering what you want that to look like. Should you continue to climb the corporate ladder, pursue a new challenge outside your current organisation or transition to a different industry altogether?

There's no one size fits all answer to these questions; all of these options present opportunities for leaders who have taken a strategic approach to mapping their career. Your next career move will depend on a variety of factors, including your personal goals, professional passions and the opportunities available to you. Here are my three key observations of the things that successful leaders do well that can become your career game changers.

Observation #1: They dedicate time and effort to the next phase of their career

High-performing leaders appreciate more than anyone that simply doing a good job counts for very little in the promotion stakes at the highest levels. Doing a good job is simply a hygiene factor that won't be enough to get you to your next senior role. New strategies are required, so recognise that and make the switch.

Many of the people I work with have always been approached and offered roles. Suddenly, they find that's no longer happening. While their success to date has not been accidental, making further progress requires a behaviour change. That means dedicating time and effort to it and you can't underestimate the importance of that. You need to approach your career strategy in the same way you would a business strategy. It's not sufficient to send out your CV or post on LinkedIn.

I regularly see how successful leaders get to the top by constantly preparing and being forward thinking and forward looking rather than relying on past experience. Yet many people continue to believe that the skills and behaviours that got them to their current level will take them to the next one. You're moving to a different level so you need a different toolkit.

I can't emphasise enough the value of mentors and sponsors. These are the people who can provide you with guidance and support as you plan and prepare for your next career move. They might be people with experience in the field you want to move into who can offer insights into a different functional area and its challenges. If your next move is likely to a new industry sector, having a mentor or a sponsor with a wider network can be invaluable.

Don't underestimate the benefits of reverse mentoring. In my experience this often gets overlooked. Being on a senior upward career trajectory, you may not appreciate the value of being reverse mentored by a younger and less experienced colleague. But the beauty of reverse mentoring is that not only can you learn a lot from your younger mentor, especially about technology and digital media, you also learn a great deal about yourself. Reverse mentoring broadens your horizons, demonstrates a growth mindset and is well worth including in your career strategy. When seeking out mentors and advisors be respectful of their time and expertise. Be clear about what you want to achieve and how they can help you on your journey.

You must also become a master of networking, seeking out and connecting with others in your industry or field who can provide valuable insights and connections. You can do this by reaching out to former colleagues, joining professional organisations to bolster your existing networks and attending events that are relevant to your interests and career goals. If you're looking to transition to a new industry, attending events and conferences to meet people in your new field and learn about the latest trends and best practices will pay dividends. You might also want to consider joining professional organisations or networking groups relevant to your new industry.

Jane is a senior marketing executive client of mine with a strong drive for professional growth but she has a degree of reluctance and some limiting beliefs relating to networking. After a few coaching sessions she decided to attend a healthcare marketing conference and made it a priority to engage with as many professionals as possible. She initiated conversations that delved into the depths of healthcare marketing and, by demonstrating thoughtful questioning and active listening, she had some meaningful exchanges that enabled her to glean insights from industry leaders.

Jane's unwavering commitment to expanding her network yielded fruitful results. Through engaging conversations, she cultivated a range of valuable connections. Notably, she met a marketing executive from a healthcare start-up actively seeking a chief marketing officer (CMO). Impressed by Jane's passion, expertise and the quality of their interaction, the start-up recognised her potential to spearhead their growth strategy.

I'm sure you'll agree that networking can unlock transformative potential. However, it must also be approached with genuine curiosity and generosity. Ask questions and listen actively to the insights and experiences of others. Share your knowledge and experience when it's relevant and helpful. Be strategic about who you connect with. Look for people who have experience in your new field and can offer valuable insights and advice. And don't be afraid to ask for introductions or reach out to people cold.

In being strategic and deliberate, you can never let the grass grow under your feet. The biggest mistake you can make when seeking your next career move is waiting to be asked. In doing so, you risk waiting too long, forgetting the importance of switching strategies and potentially missing the boat. This can be extremely frustrating, especially if you know that you're doing well, getting good performance reviews and positive employee feedback, etc. Holding back and continuing to do what you've done before, in terms of moving your career progression forward, is no longer working. Don't wait, because others won't be waiting. This is a different market with different rules and you need a different strategy for success.

If you're serious about building your network and learning how to build meaningful connections to support your career journey, I invite you to participate in my 30-day challenge. The concept is simple: engage or meet with 30 new people in 30 days. Why should you do this? Not only will it expand your network but it will also be an important opportunity for you to get used to speaking about yourself and your career. Believe me, you'll be doing that a lot and you need to be good at it if you want to reach the next phase of your career. I do the 30-day challenge three times a year and find that it not only expands my comfort zone but is also an opportunity to learn and unlearn so much.

Observation #2: They see their coach as a secret weapon

Working with a coach, whether in group coaching, leadership inner circles or one to one, can make a huge difference to your career progression. The higher you go in your career, the lonelier it can be and the more isolated it can feel. It's fiercely competitive and there are only so many roles at that level. There may be others from within your organisation who are interested in the same role. Even globally, at the highest level, you'll find yourself in a very small circle.

Working with a coach is an effective way for you to improve your self-awareness, clarify goals, encourage a growth mindset and identify growth opportunities, all of which will help accelerate your long-term career success. Your coach might play devil's advocate along the way but they're always on your side.

Coaching that aims to prepare you for your next career move might typically entail a 6- or 12-month programme. This will involve the use of various assessments and frameworks that give you a better understanding of yourself and your values, identify the optimal work environment and help you to make those subtle changes to your strategy and behaviour that are essential to fulfilling your career goals. Beyond that initial programme, many executives at the highest levels often continue to work with their coach, evolving this into a periodic arrangement, with their coach adopting more of a supportive role.

The prospect of an exciting new career move can distract you from the responsibilities of your existing role but you need to stay focused and maintain a consistently strong performance. It can be challenging; in fact, it can feel as if you're doing two jobs. It's a balancing act because both are so important. A coach can help you to strike that balance, bringing your attention back to your current role while continuing to prepare for your next one.

A coach can help you stay strategic as you navigate the challenges of making that next big career move. Let me share the experience of a client who was a senior vice president (SVP) of operations.

Alex had started his career in his current company eight years ago, progressing up the career ladder by being offered different roles, until now. He'd always focused on his career progression within the company and had never actively sought opportunities outside. After several years in his current role, he felt he'd hit a ceiling in terms of his growth and was ready for a new challenge. However, he realised he hadn't been active in building his network outside the company or developing his personal brand. So despite everyone telling him he should have no problem moving to the next phase of his career, he felt stuck. Supported by coaching, Alex developed a more strategic approach:

He reached out to former colleagues and industry contacts to build his network. He also joined industry associations and attended conferences to expand his connections. (See more about networking and influencing in PRINCIPLE 11.)

He identified areas where he wanted to build skills and experience to make himself more competitive in new roles. He volunteered for projects outside his usual scope of work and took on additional responsibilities to broaden his skill set.

He developed his personal brand by writing articles for industry publications and speaking at conferences on his area of expertise.

If your career so far has been a succession of roles that have been offered to you, you may well be feeling frustrated by the challenges of mapping out a strategy for finding your next one. I've coached some highly successful, experienced senior leaders who have been extremely hard on themselves for not knowing how to do that. The reality is, however, that in spite of their achievements this is one area in which they lack experience. After all, they will only do it so many times in a lifetime. My advice is to be kinder and more compassionate to yourself and have more realistic expectations of your knowledge and experience of the process of reaching the highest levels of senior leadership.

Observation #3: They become relevant to where they want to go

Position yourself where you want to go next, not where you've been. Basing future career goals and aspirations on past experience is a mistake that I've seen people make many times. You've achieved a great deal and know that past experience has got you to where you are now, so naturally you focus more on what you've already done. But it needs to be relevant to where you want to be in the future.

This is particularly the case for senior leaders with a lot of experience or a certain reputation. They're known for their achievements, which may have been well publicised. In these situations, it becomes easy to stay focused on that as opposed to focusing your attention on where you're going and which parts of what you've done are relevant to where you're heading. This requires a significant mindset shift for leaders who are successful at strategy but not so good at mapping out their next career move.

Look at everything you've done. Ask yourself, is this relevant to where you want to go or is it just something that you're immensely proud of? People will associate you with a standout achievement from the past but is this your ticket? This is a challenge that requires you to let go of your old identity and embrace the new identity that you aspire to, bringing only your relevant experiences with you. And remember that it's a transition that no senior leader can afford to make slowly.

When you're defining your career goals, think beyond just the next role, while keeping your relevance firmly at the forefront of your mind. Consider what you want to achieve over the long term. Be specific and realistic with your goals and ensure they align with your personal values and strengths. Once you've defined your career goals, think about how you can position yourself for success. For example, this could involve upskilling, building your network or seeking out specific types of roles or companies.

When an email dropped into my inbox from a former client, I knew he was ready for his next move. David, a CFO at a manufacturing company, was interested in transitioning to a CFO role in the technology industry. While working on his career goals, David realised that he needed to upskill in areas such as data analytics and digital transformation in order to be competitive for roles in this industry. While we continued working together, he enrolled in a data analytics course and sought out opportunities to lead digital transformation initiatives in his current role. I'm delighted to say that after nine months he proudly accepted a CFO role within a software company in London.

Taking on stretch assignments in your current role can help you build new skills and gain experience that can make you more competitive for your next career move. This is an excellent way to position yourself on your desired career path. Equally, it's an effective way of finding out that perhaps the role you were aspiring to isn't what you enjoy and going back to the drawing board to reconsider your career goals.

A stretch assignment could be an opportunity to be involved in a cultural or organisational transformation. It may involve you doing what you're doing now but in a different context. However, to stretch you, it must be something outside the typical scope of your job – for example, leading a large transformation project or being a member of the senior project management team. Any transformation project that reaches beyond your normal remit constitutes a good stretch assignment. At the CEO level, a stretch assignment could be taking an external board role or getting involved in mergers and acquisitions activity.

Identify areas where you want to build skills or gain experience that are important and relevant to the roles or industries you're interested in and look for opportunities to take on new responsibilities or lead new initiatives in your current role. Seek feedback and guidance from colleagues or mentors to help you grow in these areas. All of this will ensure that you stay relevant to where you want to go.

REFLECT AND GROW

Here are the top three key takeaways from PRINCIPLE 9:

+ *You must be strategic about your next career move because what got you here won't get you there.*

+ *Dedicate time and effort to it; it's not something you do when you have spare time. There's no need to reinvent the wheel but work with a coach to maximise impact. You don't want to miss out on an opportunity so timing is everything.*

+ *Be relevant to where you're heading and let go of the past.*

Reflect on the three points below:

+ *Spend time and energy on outlining your next career move.*

+ *Identify three strategies and integrate them into your strategy.*

+ *Share your thoughts on your career journey so far and the path ahead with a few trusted leaders and seek their perspective and feedback.*

YOUR PERFORMANCE ADVANTAGE HACK

Reflect on your career so far. Have you been strategic enough? Do you need to switch approach and shift gear?

PRINCIPLE 10

DESIGN YOUR PERSONAL BRANDING

Too many people overvalue what they are not and undervalue what they are. – Malcolm Forbes

If you have yet to prioritise the development of your personal brand, then now's the time to start. In the words of Jeff Bezos, 'Your brand is what people say about you when you're not in the room', so I urge you to see it as the most potent catalyst for building trust. It's more than just a catchy phrase; your personal brand is critical to your leadership and career success. And I'm sure you'll agree that you need to be clear about what you'd like others to say about you when you're not in the room. An authentic personal brand is one of your most impactful marginal gains to your success because it demonstrates what you stand for, what you're seeking and the value that you want to add.

To put it simply, you have two choices: you either let others say what they want, based on their perceptions, or consciously drive the process and ensure that what others say about you, both online and offline, aligns closely with your image. Because if you're not branding yourself, you can be sure that others will be doing it for you and you'll end up constantly trying to outperform your image and feeling misunderstood. Or you may not get the chance to perform at all because of your image. Don't be complacent and think that doing a good job is sufficient at your level. You'll simply remain the best-kept secret. Don't leave your success to chance by making your personal branding accidental; it could be the biggest opportunity cost of your leadership and career success.

I have a confession to make: I'm not immune to not paying enough attention to my personal brand. In fact, I'd been running my business for several years before I took my own advice, the same advice that I give to my clients, and that was to ask 100 people in my network, 'What were the first three words that came to mind when you thought of me?' To my great surprise they all replied quickly but my initial joy disappeared when I saw that every single message, without fail, included the word 'power'. I was shocked and, if I'm honest, mortified.

I couldn't believe that everybody had misunderstood me so badly. I'm the last person to want to seek power; my time and energy are dedicated to sharing to inspire. After a tough 48 hours I tapped into my resilience to move forward and decided to call a few people and face reality. I was curious about their initial thinking and how they had come up with the word power because clearly I'd been doing something terribly wrong. Then all became clear as the people I called told me that they had chosen the word to mean empowering and powerful at the same time. That was something I could live with. That was also the moment when the brand AC PowerCoaching was born. And when I finally announced it at a large conference I was inundated with messages saying, 'Finally! Did you not know that we have been calling you the power coach for quite a while?'

Personal branding is not just for entrepreneurs or influencers; it's an integral part of a leader's career success. Early on in your career, you were promoted or offered the next role because you did a good job and because of your competencies. As you progress to the next career stage, it matters who you know but it also matters who knows you and what comes to mind when they see your name on meeting lists, events or social media, or most importantly when considering who to invite to the table. Your personal brand precedes you and remains in the room after you leave. As a leader, you need to differentiate yourself from others and create a unique and consistent image of yourself that others can easily recognise and remember. Personal branding is the key to that.

What is personal branding?

Personal branding has become something of a buzzword in recent years, especially in business and leadership circles. It refers to creating a unique and consistent image of oneself that others can associate with. But personal branding is much more than just having a good reputation. It's about being strategic, intentional and purposeful in how you present yourself to others and is essential for high-performing senior leaders. Simply put, your personal brand is the way people see you – everything from your skills and expertise to your achievements and the way you present yourself. Whether online or offline, you already have a personal brand. The key is to make sure that your brand represents you the way you want it to.

Building a personal brand isn't something you can do and then set aside for months or years. It's an ongoing commitment to actively promoting yourself and your skill set, engaging with followers across multiple channels to maintain a positive online reputation. Developing a personal brand takes time and effort but, like finding your superpower, it will be one of the best long-term investments you ever make. I want you to see it as the intentional process of establishing and promoting your unique identity and reputation that differentiates you from others in your industry or field. It involves leveraging your skills, strengths, values and personality to build a recognisable and trustworthy brand that attracts followers, creates opportunities and makes a positive impact.

Effective personal branding will help you establish yourself as a thought leader, enhance your influence and credibility and create a lasting legacy. It will also help you to navigate challenges and setbacks, as a strong personal brand can provide a foundation of trust and support from followers and stakeholders. Some of the most influential leaders have taken the positive impact of their personal brand to new levels.

I truly admire the way that research professor Brené Brown has built a personal brand focused on vulnerability, courage and empathy. She has conducted extensive research on these topics and written several bestselling books, including *Daring Greatly* (2012) and *Braving the*

Wilderness (2017). From a personal branding perspective, she says that exposing our thoughts and flaws, becoming more vulnerable in our talks and presentations, in podcast interviews and in the content we produce, is a brilliant way to connect emotionally with your audience.

Meanwhile, Virgin Group founder Richard Branson has used his personal brand to create a strong image as a risk-taker and adventurer. In doing so he has emphasised the importance of innovation and entrepreneurship through his brand, which has helped him to attract customers and investors across a variety of industries.

Personal branding comprises various elements, such as creating a compelling message or mission statement, developing a strong online and offline presence, communicating with clarity and authenticity and building relationships with key stakeholders. It's not about being self-promoting or superficial but rather about building a reputation that's authentic, consistent and aligned with one's values and goals.

As a leader, you need to differentiate yourself from others and create a unique and consistent image of yourself that others can easily recognise and remember. It is of course, critical for your next career move but is often overlooked as a great catalyst and trust builder for leading organisational transformation.

What are the benefits of having a strong personal brand?

Personal branding involves strategically presenting yourself to others by showcasing your skills, strengths and values in order to stand out from the crowd. This builds trust, credibility and influence with your audience. When you have a strong personal brand, people perceive you as credible and knowledgeable, leading to better opportunities and relationships.

And let's not forget about influence – your ability to persuade and motivate others to take action. Your personal branding helps to strengthen your influence by creating a strong and memorable impression. When you have a strong personal brand, people are more likely to be influenced by your ideas and recommendations.

Personal branding also makes you more visible in your industry and sector. When you have a strong personal brand, you're more likely to be recognised and remembered by others, which can lead to new opportunities, collaborations and partnerships.

Finally, personal branding helps to create a positive image, which has a profound impact on the way that people perceive and respond to you. Developing and promoting your personal brand is an ongoing process of refining and strengthening your image. As a leader, it's a valuable asset, so take good care of it.

How to design your personal brand

Remember that your brand differentiates you and helps you stand out from the crowd. When you're intentional about your personal brand, it attracts the right audience and opportunities and people know what they can expect from you. As you start thinking more consciously about the concept, I want you to consider a few practical aspects on the way.

Define your personal brand: Identify your core values, key strengths and unique value proposition. Reflect on your strengths, accomplishments and professional goals and ask yourself, 'What makes me stand out in my industry?'

Create a personal brand statement: This is how you communicate your brand identity and value proposition, so your key messaging must be clear, concise and memorable.

Build your online presence: This is fundamental for creating and maintaining a strong personal brand. Create a professional website, social media profiles and other digital assets that will best showcase your expertise and thought leadership.

Share your thought leadership: Now you need to establish your authority and credibility in your industry by sharing it through various channels, including blog posts, articles and speeches.

Network effectively: Make the time to attend industry events, join professional organisations and engage with your peers and stakeholders. Build relationships and collaborate with others to build your personal brand and expand your influence.

Observations

I firmly believe that every high-performing and successful leader should focus on building a strong personal brand to help them establish their authority, build trust and enhance their reputation. This isn't about creating a fancy logo or a catchy tagline. It's about defining your unique value proposition, communicating your expertise and showcasing your thought leadership. A strong personal brand helps you differentiate yourself from your competitors and stand out in a crowded market. As someone once quipped, 'Be yourself; everyone else is already taken.'

Personal branding has been the most in-demand leadership inner circles programme and retreat that I have run in the past five years. It's a popular topic with executives during their one-to-one coaching sessions and features prominently in my leadership training courses. Therefore I'd like to share three important observations of leaders who have mastered the power of personal branding for their career and leadership success.

Observation #1: They have a personal brand strategy

People often think that a personal brand is something that happens to you as a result of doing a good job or by working for a certain organisation. They think the larger and more recognised the organisation, the stronger their personal brand will be. But that's not their personal brand – it's their organisation's brand.

A good indicator of the strength of your personal brand is the number of events you'd be invited to if you didn't have your organisation or job title. Leaders are often surprised to find that when they switch organisations or retire that the number of invitations they receive drops by as much as 80 per cent. That's when they realise that previous invitations were received because of the role they played in the organisation and not because of their personal brand.

Leadership coach Marshall Goldsmith is a keen advocate of getting feedback to build authentic personal branding. He believes that feedback can help leaders identify gaps in understanding and areas for improvement. However, that feedback can sometimes come from the most unexpected sources.

Like many leaders, I encountered the perplexing challenge of distilling my personal brand into a succinct sentence. It was a struggle to capture the essence of who I was and what I stood for in a concise manner. Little did I know that an unexpected encounter at the Savoy Hotel in London would serve as a pivotal moment in shaping my understanding of my own personal brand.

Following our meeting, my client expressed a desire to meet my son. As they engaged in a light-hearted conversation, my client playfully posed a question to my son, asking, 'What does your mother do, anyway?' To my astonishment, my son, without hesitation, looked up at him and replied, 'My mommy makes people think differently.'

It wasn't something I'd ever said to him; it was simply what he'd observed. I realised that was what others said about me but I'd been unaware of it. So my advice is, don't shy away from taking feedback on personal branding from non-experts. This shouldn't be limited to experts or professionals alone. Non-experts, in their genuine observations, often provide valuable insights that can illuminate aspects of our personal brand that may have been overlooked.

Personal branding requires a strategy and creating that strategy is a process rather than a collection of accidental activities. Start by building your emotional inventory. Listen to the voice in your head and ask how you want people to feel when interacting with you and how you want people to talk about you. Set out your plan and vision for the next six months, twelve months, three years and, most importantly, think about what could potentially stop you from fulfilling that vision.

Think about your audience. The people you hope to serve or attract are your audience and all your brand communication will come back to them. Your message and brand won't connect with everyone, so define a group or cohort you want to serve. This will help you to measure how your brand message is impacting your intended audience.

Identify your target audience's core needs, not just on a physical level but also on an emotional level. For example, they might need to feel safe or they may want a quick solution for healthy eating. The impact your brand has on people should be intentional and purposeful.

You know the attributes of your personal brand and your audience's needs. Now you can create your brand mission statement and every piece of your branding will come back to this, from the way you talk to your audience to the articles you share with them. It also has to be authentic because it's the way you'll show up for your audience. Authenticity is the key to building trust and connection and your brand's mission will encourage your audience to want to know more. Ask yourself, 'Is this mission authentic to me and my values?' If necessary, change the mission so that you can apply it consistently.

In simple terms, a **push strategy** involves putting posts on LinkedIn. It can be an effective marketing strategy but it's not my recommended one for senior leaders. Much more effective is the **pull strategy**, which attracts attention, inspires and creates that desire from your audience, who will form an opinion of you, your values, what you stand for, your skills and expertise. There's nothing wrong with wanting to communicate about what you've been doing, for example, speaking at a high-profile event, but it requires subtlety, so maybe refer to it within a thought leadership post rather than making it the main thrust of the post itself.

The higher you go as a senior leader, the more visible you become, so it's crucial to create and nurture those brand attributes that people engage with and demonstrate your authenticity and focus on what you want people to think about you when you're not in the room.

Observation #2: They know that their personal brand is a work in progress

Your personal brand must relate to where you're going, not where you've been. This requires you to be extremely proactive in maintaining your brand. It's important to follow up the process of developing your personal brand by continuing to further evolve and adapt your business identity.

If your industry changes, reflecting those changes can be a valuable tool in your marketing efforts, further demonstrating your ability to be current, relevant and knowledgeable. Your customers and potential employers' tastes and preferences are also likely to change over time, so you'll need to be constantly observing and ensuring that your personal brand is relevant for the stage you're at in your career journey.

As your career progresses over time, your core brand may not change. What will change is how you manifest it and that may differ depending on what's happening within your organisation or job role. So how do you navigate this sensitively and proactively? Your goal is to be seen as a person, not as a role, an organisation or a function. What you don't want is for people to associate you with your current organisation. That is your organisation's brand.

As with the design process, maintaining your personal brand shouldn't take place in isolation. Aba and I have known each other for about five years. We'd been connected on various social media channels and she'd attended some of my masterclasses when she approached me for coaching. At this point she had been working in the same leadership role for several years. She aspired to advance her career and an internal opportunity came up for an SVP position. However, she recognised that her personal brand wasn't aligned with her career goals. So we embarked on a journey together to review her personal brand following a roadmap, which you may also find useful.

Seeking feedback: Aba isn't afraid to seek feedback from all corners, including her colleagues, mentors and even her subordinates and truly values the diverse perspectives they bring. She makes constructive criticism a valuable ally, providing invaluable insights into how others perceive her and shedding light on areas where she can refine her professional image.

Creating a strong online presence: Aba meticulously evaluates her professional profiles on platforms such as LinkedIn, ensuring that her online persona aligns harmoniously with her desired personal brand. Every detail, from her bio to her headline and the content she shares reflects her expertise, achievements and the values she holds dear.

Communicating consistently: This is Aba's secret weapon in effectively communicating her personal brand. She pays close attention to her interactions across various channels (in meetings, presentations or written communication) and weaves her messaging to align seamlessly with her intended brand image. Her words are clear, her ideas concise and she conveys her unique value proposition in a way that captivates others.

Ongoing professional development: Aba identifies specific areas for growth and seeks opportunities to strengthen her personal brand, from attending relevant workshops and pursuing advanced certifications to immersing herself in new experiences that stretch her skills. With each step, she enhances her credibility, deepens her expertise and widens the horizon of her personal brand.

Quality not quantity: Aba knows that building a network isn't just about the quantity of connections but the quality of relationships. She actively engages in networking activities, industry conferences and meaningful forums, seeking opportunities to connect with other influential leaders in her field. By fostering a strong network, she expands her knowledge base and reinforces her personal brand through positive interactions with others.

Leveraging thought leadership: Aba leverages her expertise and insights to leave an indelible mark in her industry, sharing her knowledge by writing thought-provoking articles, speaking at prestigious conferences and even hosting webinars. By contributing valuable content and showcasing her expertise, she establishes herself as an authority, further amplifying her personal brand.

Observation #3: Their personal brand is authentic, consistent and easy to connect with

Authenticity is the key to building a strong, believable brand that people want to connect with. Be true to yourself, stay grounded in the values of your personal brand and avoid trying to be somebody else. Focus on your strengths and areas of expertise and differentiate yourself from others within your industry or peer group to build that credibility and influence, which links strongly to your personal brand. I'll share more about influence in PRINCIPLE 11.

Build relationships with key stakeholders. That's an important part of manifesting your brand and building that brand beyond your existing organisation and regular peer group. Communicating with empathy is critical. Whether it's online or offline, on social media or during interviews, come back to that crucial question: what is your message? What are those three words that you want people to say about you when you're not in the room?

Thought leadership is a powerful way of manifesting your personal brand. It doesn't necessarily mean writing weekly posts or planning to write a book. It doesn't have to mean endless work that consumes too much of your thinking time. However, I'm a firm believer that leaders create leaders and thought leadership is where a huge amount of influence lies. It allows you to demonstrate your expertise and allows others to get to know you within the context of your personal brand. When you're a thought leader, you engage with and inspire others and it can be a vital asset in the process of moving your career forward.

Don't underestimate the importance of digital technology to your personal brand. Embracing tech can be challenging but if you want to maximise the impact and influence of your personal brand, you must take ownership of it. You don't have to be active on every single platform and channel; be selective and identify what's relevant to where you're going. This will keep you up to date and on trend and will allow you to connect your personal brand with a much wider audience.

Authenticity isn't a luxury; it's a strategic advantage. When you authentically connect with others, you build trust, foster collaboration and inspire loyalty. I recently had the privilege of working with a CEO who was known for her authentic leadership style. She genuinely cared about her employees' wellbeing and openly acknowledged her own mistakes, learning from them alongside her team. Through her vulnerability, she created an environment where everyone felt valued, contributing to a culture of high performance and employee satisfaction.

Time and time again I've seen how authenticity begins with self-awareness. It's about understanding your strengths, values and aspirations. By aligning your personal brand with these core elements, you create an authentic presence that resonates with others.

Remember that authenticity is a lifelong journey of self-discovery and growth. By consistently leading with authenticity, you'll not only create a personal brand that stands out but also one that inspires those around you to embrace their own authentic selves. You'll undoubtedly enable others to trust and connect with you quickly, which is an absolute must if you're in an interview, networking or leading a transformation.

REFLECT AND GROW

Here are the top three key takeaways from PRINCIPLE 10:

+ *Your personal brand is what others think and say about you when you're not there.*

+ *Dedicate time and effort to designing and understanding your personal brand.*

+ *Recognise that your personal brand isn't static and must represent the authentic you to be impactful.*

Reflect on the three points below:

+ *How do you want others to see you when you're not in the room?*

+ *What steps will you take to design and or review your personal brand?*

+ *Who is your target audience for your brand?*

YOUR PERFORMANCE ADVANTAGE HACK

Ask 20 others in your network to message you with the first three words that come to mind when they think of you.

PRINCIPLE 11

LEVERAGE THE POWER OF YOUR INFLUENCE

People do not buy goods and services. They buy relations, stories and magic. – Seth Godin

As you advance in your career, a significant aspect of your leadership revolves around your ability to influence. Have you recently taken the time to reflect on how you influence others? The process of influencing doesn't begin when you're faced with leading your team, organisation or stakeholders through a transformation, for example. It starts way before that, with genuinely showing interest in those around you and forging connections and relationships built on trust.

Authenticity is, however, paramount in this endeavour. Merely engaging in short-term, self-serving interactions may appear impactful momentarily but, in truth, it fails to influence anyone. True leadership lies in cultivating genuine connections, trust and ensuring lasting influence through sincere engagement with others.

Today, Alice is one of my coaching clients. However, in 2020, she was a participant in the UN Mastermind Group for Sustainable Development, a ground-breaking collaborative programme that I led and co-designed in collaboration with UNSSC (United Nations Systems Staff College). Initially, Alice introduced herself to her fellow masterminds as the regional director for Africa in an international organisation dedicated to wildlife preservation. Yet beyond her responsibilities and remarkable career achievements, there was something about her that truly inspired me.

She's a passionate, driven and energetic individual. Her extensive experience and expertise make her truly unique. She embodies authenticity, and as a proud mother of two wonderful girls, whom I've had the privilege to meet, her core values shine through. I had the opportunity to witness her compassionate and transformational leadership first hand while we worked on two interconnected projects. One aimed to engage a diverse group of stakeholders while the other focused on empowering staff leadership.

Whether you've met Alice in person, interacted with her online or simply followed her on social media, you'll immediately sense her genuine care and trustworthiness. These qualities form the foundation of her influential abilities. She's innovative, bold and compassionate to her core – a combination she consistently demonstrates and undoubtedly serves as her influencing superpower.

However, influencing isn't just about using the right strategies but about doing your homework. You don't need the same level of trust, connection and relationship with everyone; that would be energy draining and have little impact. However, if you want to use the power of influence to elevate your leadership and career, then you need to be deliberate and laser focused on how you relate to others. True leadership extends beyond mere authority. It encompasses the power to effect change, motivate teams and drive organisational success.

Knowing someone's name even if they don't know yours doesn't establish trust but it's an important first step towards building a connection. And it doesn't stop there. Influencing shouldn't look like tightrope walking. Rather, it should be visualised as surfing: adopting a big-picture perspective and taking an interest in others can be compared with getting to know the waves before deciding to commit and start surfing. Influencing takes many shapes and forms and serves several purposes as a leadership career tool.

Effective leaders understand how to inspire and influence others by tapping into their aspirations and motivating them to pursue a shared vision. By connecting with individuals on a deeper level and appealing to their sense of purpose, they can drive significant change and achieve remarkable results. The story of Steve Jobs and John Sculley is a perfect illustration of this.

I always think back to the early 1980s, when Steve Jobs, co-founder and CEO of Apple Inc., was looking for a new CEO to lead the company. At the time, Apple was facing declining sales and market share. Jobs had a vision for Apple's future but he knew he needed a strong leader who could turn the company around and bring his vision to life. He came across a talented executive named John Sculley, then the CEO of PepsiCo, whose marketing expertise and leadership skills Jobs believed could help transform Apple into a consumer electronics powerhouse. He decided to recruit Sculley to join Apple.

Jobs flew to New York to meet him and convince him to leave PepsiCo. During their meeting, Jobs asked Sculley a powerful question that would ultimately sway his decision. He said, 'Do you want to spend the rest of your life selling sugared water or do you want a chance to change the world?' This question had a profound impact on Sculley. It made him reflect on his career and the impact he could have by joining Apple. He was inspired by Jobs' vision of creating innovative and user-friendly technology that could revolutionise the world. Ultimately, Sculley made the difficult decision to leave PepsiCo and join Apple as CEO in 1983.

With Sculley's leadership and Jobs' visionary guidance, Apple flourished, launching flagship products such as the Macintosh computer and growing its market share significantly. Although their relationship later soured and Sculley was eventually replaced as CEO, this story highlights Jobs' exceptional ability to influence others. By posing a thought-provoking question that appealed to Sculley's desire for a greater purpose, Jobs persuaded him to join Apple and contribute to its success.

How do you influence? Perhaps through masterful questioning, your experience and expertise or relying on personal qualities? Successful leaders are strategic in their use of influence to inspire change, shape industries and impact society. Whatever journey you're on, mastering the art of influencing should be a priority.

It doesn't start with you announcing your organisation's new transformation strategy; your influence began long before that. Give before you get, be mindful and never underestimate the time you need to take to understand others and their context. If you demonstrate generosity and selflessness, you build trust and goodwill with your team or stakeholders, making them more receptive to your ideas and guidance. By understanding their context, challenges and aspirations, you can tailor your approach and decision making to better support their growth and success. Most importantly, nail your influencing style and strategies, because perhaps 80 per cent of your leadership is about your ability to influence.

Influencing in practice

For high-performing leaders who aspire to reach the pinnacle of success, the ability to influence others is paramount. As George Hallenbeck once said (2016), 'Without the capacity to influence others, your ability to make what you envision a reality remains elusive because, after all, no one can do it alone. Without the ability to influence the hearts, minds and energy of others, the truly important things in work and in life can't be achieved.'

Influence is a powerful tool. The ability to sway opinions, motivate others and inspire change and transformation is a defining characteristic of successful leaders. From visionaries who transformed industries to political leaders who rallied nations, these individuals harnessed the power of influence to shape the world around them.

When devising a strategy for being influential you need to incorporate several key elements:

Building relationships: One of the foundations of effective influencing is building strong relationships. Successful leaders invest time and effort in developing connections with their team members and stakeholders. By building trust and rapport, you'll gain credibility and enhance your ability to influence others. By cultivating meaningful connections, you'll create a solid foundation for your influence.

Sheryl Sandberg exemplifies this phenomenon. Her book, *Lean In*, is a testament to her exceptional skill in connecting with diverse individuals and motivating them to embrace diversity while pursuing their aspirations. Through her valuable connections, Sandberg has emerged as a prominent influencer in the technology industry and a passionate champion of women's empowerment.

Communicating with clarity: Nelson Mandela was renowned for his powerful and persuasive communication skills. During his imprisonment, he wrote numerous letters and delivered speeches that conveyed his unwavering commitment to justice, equality and a unified South Africa. His words resonated deeply with people, both within the country and around the world, inspiring hope and igniting a movement against apartheid. Mandela's influential communication played a crucial role in garnering support for the anti-apartheid struggle, leading to international pressure on the South African government and eventual negotiations for a democratic transition.

Clear communication is crucial for effective influencing, as is the ability to articulate ideas and visions in a compelling and easy to understand manner. Your communication style must resonate with different audiences, which requires the use of storytelling, visuals and persuasive language to convey your message.

Leading by example: Actions speak louder than words. This is a principle that every successful leader understands. You must lead by example, demonstrating the values and behaviours that you expect from your followers. By embodying your vision and principles, you'll inspire others to adopt the same mindset and approach. When you lead by example, you create a powerful ripple effect. Your actions serve as a source of inspiration, motivating those around you to strive for excellence and embrace the same values that drive you. This form of leadership transcends verbal directives and empowers individuals to witness first hand the impact of your beliefs and choices.

By consistently demonstrating integrity, accountability and dedication, you set the bar high for others to follow. Your commitment to your vision establishes a standard of excellence that permeates throughout the team or organisation. People are naturally drawn to leaders who practise what they preach and they find solace and trust in knowing that their leader walks the talk.

Leading by example isn't limited to professional endeavours alone; it extends to personal conduct as well. When you embody your values in all aspects of your life, you create a harmonious alignment that resonates with those around you. Whether it's cultivating a supportive and inclusive work environment, promoting work–life integration or displaying empathy and compassion, your actions inspire others to do the same. It's important to remember that leading by example is an ongoing commitment. Consistency is key.

Building coalitions and alliances: It's important to recognise the power of collaboration and forming alliances and to understand that bringing together diverse perspectives and expertise amplifies their influence and the ability to achieve collective goals. When you bring together individuals and organisations from different backgrounds, industries and disciplines, you tap into a wealth of knowledge, skills and experiences. This diversity enriches your understanding of complex issues and widens the range of solutions available. By incorporating multiple viewpoints, you can develop more comprehensive strategies and approaches that address the various dimensions of a problem. This inclusive process not only strengthens the quality of your decisions but also increases the likelihood of successful implementation.

I often see how it cultivates a sense of shared ownership and collective responsibility. When individuals and organisations come together around a common vision, they feel a greater sense of commitment and investment in the outcome. This shared purpose fuels motivation and dedication, resulting in increased collaboration and a higher likelihood of achieving desired outcomes. Most importantly, whatever strategy you choose, make it your own, be genuine and remember that influencing is not a one-off transaction.

Observations

Leadership isn't about position or title but about influence. While power may change hands as executives transition or organisations evolve, influence has the potential for enduring impact. When you cultivate strong relationships, you inspire others and promote a positive organisational culture that leaves a lasting legacy and transcends your formal authority. Your influence can continue to shape the organisation's trajectory long after you've moved on.

Power can be an important tool for leaders but influence ultimately enables them to mobilise teams, drive change and achieve sustainable success. Influence empowers you to go beyond the constraints of formal authority, connecting with individuals on a deeper level and inspiring them to contribute their best. By cultivating influence, you can create a positive work environment, foster collaboration, navigate change effectively and leave a lasting impact on your organisation, its culture and its future success.

How do high-performing leaders change people's perspectives so they can make an empowered decision, achieve strategic alignment and influence others *not* to do something?

Observation #1: They don't network, they build relationships

Leaders who are skilled at influencing others recognise and cultivate the power of networks. Organisations are increasingly dynamic, morphing in size and shape over time. Influential leaders recognise that their personal networks must also be dynamic and they continually grow and strengthen their networks. They're also strategic about choosing how and when to tap into this network.

People often comment on the size of my network yet the truth is I don't network. Instead, I take a genuine interest in others. My focus is on them and not what they can do for me and this becomes a source of influence. I've observed successful leaders who take a similar approach. It's a process; you connect, you take an interest, you establish an initial connection and you start building trust. Maintaining those relationships is critical.

That all sounds straightforward in the physical world but this is the digital age; how you do build the same relationships online? The process is exactly the same. You start by looking at their flow. What are they interested in? You might start by following them on social media, reading their posts and blogs, offering your comments and then making a request to connect. All the while you're building a sense of trust and connection until ultimately they reciprocate because now they're interested in you and the idea of forging a relationship with you.

Building relationships online is never about numbers. It's about the quality of your connections. Having 3,000 active contacts in your online networks who know who you are and have a relationship with you is far more significant, from an influence perspective, than having 100,000 contacts whom you don't know and rarely interact with. When making those initial approaches and requesting connections, avoid using automatic direct messaging. Would you say the same thing, word for word, to everybody you meet in a physical network environment? A short, personal and pertinent message will have the desired effect. When you're connecting with people it has to be based on a genuine interest and a genuine connection.

I first crossed paths with Alison, my developmental editor, on Twitter several years ago. It all began with a hashtag I posted, sparking a conversation that revealed our surprising number of shared connections. Our online interaction eventually transcended the digital realm as we had the pleasure of meeting in London on multiple occasions. Noteworthy among these encounters were our memorable conversations held at the illustrious American Bar in the Savoy, accompanied by my favourite cocktail: Moonwalk. In case you're wondering, this cherished cocktail, attributed to the ingenuity of bartender Joe Gilmore, is rumoured to have been the first drink served to the Apollo 11 crew upon their triumphant return to Earth. As our connection deepened, Alison visited me in Bonn, the city I now call home, strengthening our bond further. Somewhere along this remarkable journey, we made a pact: if the time ever came for me to write a book, Alison would accompany me on this literary expedition.

Maintaining your relationships doesn't mean that you have to speak to people regularly. There are subtle ways of showing your awareness of what they're doing and showing care and interest. When you make an authentic connection it becomes the foundation for the rest of the relationship.

Trust is the cornerstone of effective influencing. Trust will enable you to unlock the full potential of your teams. By appreciating vulnerability, inspiring others and striking a balance between pushing boundaries and attentive listening, you can promote an environment of trust. And through open communication, consistency, empathy, accountability and collaboration, you can lay the foundation for strong and successful teams. Embrace the power of trust and witness the transformative impact it has on your leadership journey.

Without trust, you may be able to enforce compliance but you'll never unlock the full commitment, capabilities and creativity that a group can offer. When faced with daunting challenges or strategic changes, the ability to leverage these invaluable assets becomes paramount, underscoring the vital importance of trust.

Trust involves striking a delicate balance between encouraging individuals to venture beyond their comfort zones and actively listening to their concerns and feedback. Trustworthy leaders are skilful at managing the 'balancing acts' that frequently arise, for example balancing toughness and empathy. And it's crucial to recognise the challenges that individuals face during times of transition and demonstrate urgency while maintaining patience as change progresses.

Observation #2: They spend disproportionate amounts of time 'doing their homework'

Preparation and observation can never be considered a waste of time but when it comes to influence, they will be your best friends. You need to be clear about who you want to influence and, with a sound grasp of organisational intelligence, be able to identify the people who know how to get things done and embrace the reality of working within organisational politics to move teams and important initiatives forward. All organisations have two sides: the formal structure, as depicted on the organisational chart; and the informal structure, often a more accurate picture of how things really get done. Politically savvy leaders understand both aspects and view politics as a neutral and necessary part of organisational life that can be used constructively and ethically to advance organisational aims.

Emotionally intelligent individuals excel in social competence and navigate complex social dynamics with finesse. They possess a deep understanding of human emotions and can skilfully engage in effective communication. They also possess a unique understanding of the mechanisms that drive human behaviour and have the power to evoke desired effects. Take the time to assess your impact on those around you and strive to cultivate an environment of understanding, support and growth. Remember, true leadership lies not only in achieving personal success but also in empowering others.

I've always considered Iman to be an exceptional leader who embraces the power of emotional intelligence to influence and understand her team. So I was delighted when she shared with me how she navigated a tricky and challenging situation when her team member, Jean, found himself disengaged and struggling to meet deadlines. But instead of resorting to traditional disciplinary measures, Iman decided to take a different path, one that led to empathy, connection and remarkable transformation.

She invited Jean to a private meeting in a safe space where open and honest dialogue could flourish. She became fully present, actively listening as Jean shared his frustrations, challenges and underlying emotions. Every word he spoke became a valuable clue that helped Iman unravel the true essence of Jean's struggles.

This is where Iman's emotional intelligence truly shone. Rather than brushing off Jean's concerns, she wholeheartedly acknowledged his feelings, validating his experiences. With genuine care and appreciation for Jean's dedication and skills, Iman created a powerful connection, a bond that fostered trust and mutual understanding. Jean felt seen, heard and valued, realising that he was an integral part of the team.

Together, Iman and Jean embarked on a collaborative journey of problem solving. Instead of imposing her own solutions, Iman treated Jean as an equal partner, inviting him to contribute his ideas and perspectives. Through this shared brainstorming process, Jean's motivation was reignited, fuelling his desire to take ownership of his challenges and explore innovative solutions.

Throughout their conversations, Iman remained composed, regulating her own emotions and ensuring that negativity and judgement never infiltrated their interaction. Her calm and supportive demeanour set the stage for an environment of open dialogue, trust and psychological safety to thrive.

I want Iman's story to be a source of inspiration for you. Embrace the power of emotional intelligence in your own leadership journey and witness the remarkable transformations it can bring, forging meaningful connections, promoting growth and unlocking the full potential of your team through effective influencing.

Emotionally intelligent leaders understand how to harness their influence positively, creating an environment of trust, collaboration and growth. Therefore it's important to gauge your effectiveness as a leader and reflect on the impact you have on those in your presence. Consider the following questions:

+ How do people feel in your presence?
+ What are their reactions when you engage with them?
+ Are you greeted with respect, fear, stiffness, warmth or open body language?
+ Do people feel relieved to see you?

+ How often do they seek your advice or opinion?
+ When was the last time someone asked for your help?

According to Daniel Goleman (2018), emotional intelligence has four key aspects: self-awareness, self-management, social awareness and relationship management. 'Self-awareness and social awareness refer to *what we know about ourselves and others*; self-management and relationship management are *what we do with that information*,' he writes (his emphasis).

If you really want to make a difference, go back to the core and ask yourself, 'Am I tapping into my emotional intelligence? Am I maximising, for example, emotional balance or organisational happiness?' Try selecting one aspect of emotional intelligence that you'd like to focus on to further enhance your ability to be a high-performing leader. Identify another aspect that you would like your team to focus on in the next three to six months.

Observation #3: They recognise their influencing superpower and have a strategy

As a senior leader, you'll have to navigate complex networks of stakeholders and decision makers to achieve your organisational objectives. To be truly influential you'll need to invest time in understanding your stakeholders' needs, motivations and concerns, build strategic alliances, negotiate effectively and communicate your vision in a manner that resonates with key decision makers. By leveraging your network and influence, you become an advocate for your team, driving change and garnering support for critical initiatives. Regardless of industry, culture or context, I recognise three key behaviours that effective influencers consistently demonstrate:

1. thinking before responding, considering context and goals before deciding when and how to express themselves

2. paying close attention to nonverbal cues, practising active listening, considering how others might feel and finding ways to appeal to the common good

3. leaving people with a good impression without coming across as 'trying too hard'.

What's the basis of your influence? Your expertise, your network connections, your future potential? Or is it your vision or your energy? When you have a clear understanding of the foundations of influencing, you can develop and refine your influencing skills more effectively. This knowledge allows you to leverage the right strategies, approaches and techniques to influence others in a positive and impactful way.

Then you're ready to focus on who you're influencing. Mendelow's (1991) stakeholder mapping power/interest framework provides you with invaluable insight into the influencing of stakeholders, which is often a challenge and can cause many sleepless nights for a leader.

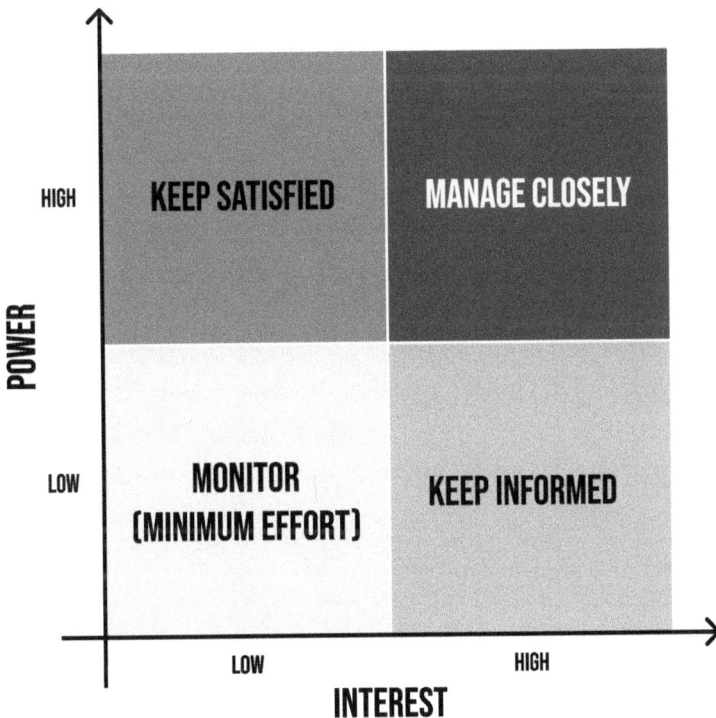

Figure 8: The power/interest stakeholder framework

Take a closer look at the four quadrants of the framework above and consider their implications. Your primary focus should be on individuals who possess high power and high interest. However, be cautious not to overwhelm stakeholders, as this can backfire, particularly with individuals who hold high power but lack significant interest. Remember, they don't need to know every single detail. It's not about what you want to convey; providing excessive information may actually influence them negatively. Equally important are individuals with low power but high interest. Be mindful not to mistake their interest for decision-making power and influence. Neglecting to allocate enough time to engage with these individuals can result in missed opportunities for influence.

Finally, don't dismiss those in the low power and low interest category. Continuously monitor their status because stakeholders can change over time. Stay vigilant and be ready to adapt your approach as circumstances evolve.

Remember, this framework isn't set in stone and requires regular review and adaptation. Let me share a real life example to illustrate this point. One of my clients, a prominent global organisation headquartered in Africa, approached me for a stakeholder consultancy session. They had previously conducted an analysis and created a stakeholder map but here's the catch — it was a decade old. Think about it: how much could have changed in that time? How many new leaders have emerged and how many previous influencers have moved on? Influencing is all about building relationships, which is why it's crucial to consistently remap your stakeholders.

By keeping your stakeholder analysis up to date, you gain valuable insights into the current landscape. You can identify key decision makers, understand their interests and concerns and tailor your approach accordingly. This proactive approach allows you to nurture relationships, adapt your influencing strategies and seize new opportunities as they arise. Don't let your stakeholder map gather dust. Regularly revisit and refresh it to reflect the ever-changing dynamics of your organisation or project. By doing so, you'll stay ahead of the curve and maintain a competitive edge in the realm of influence.

The stakeholder management power/interest framework gives you a sense of direction and a subtlety that, together with your communication and personal branding, will help you develop a strategy for effective influencing. It will dramatically change your perspective on how to manage your stakeholders, build your strategy, understand your basis for influencing and know who you're influencing.

REFLECT AND GROW

Here are the three key takeaways from PRINCIPLE 11:

+ *At this stage of your career, your leadership is largely about your ability to influence.*

+ *Influencing starts with you taking an interest in others around you and building connections and relationships to secure trust. Have a strategy and know your influencing superpower.*

+ *Prepare and observe; it's not a waste of time but your best friend when it comes to influencing.*

Reflect on the three points below:

+ *How do you influence? Reflect on the difference between your online and offline strategy.*

+ *Consider how you will use the power/interest framework as a basis for your influencing strategy.*

+ *Identify one new aspect of influencing that you will try out. Be specific in your response.*

YOUR PERFORMANCE ADVANTAGE HACK

Actively listen and seek to understand others before trying to be understood. When you genuinely listen to other's perspectives, needs and concerns, it demonstrates respect and empathy. By understanding their viewpoints, you can tailor your approach, communicate more effectively and find common ground to build upon. This approach fosters trust, opens doors for collaboration and increases the likelihood of successfully influencing.

PRINCIPLE 12

DRIVE SUCCESSFUL TRANSFORMATIONS

Anyone can hold the helm when the sea is calm.
– Publilius Syrus

Successfully leading transformation and change requires a mindset shift. But where does this shift come from and why is it so critical? Whichever way you want to look at it, as a senior leader, change, transformation and leading in uncertainty and crisis will be the key catalysts in your leadership and career success. As entrepreneur Jeff Henderson puts it, 'You have to finish well.' You have to do it every day. This gives you a huge opportunity to create a legacy and a lasting impact, not just at the organisational level but also for those you lead and influence, including all your stakeholders. The secret to successful change and transformation is you and your leadership.

This is arguably the biggest challenge you'll face. However, leading transformation is not always about the strategy. It comes down to how you lead yourself when everybody is watching you and expecting you to deliver in a sensitive and tense environment. Whether it's about growth, innovation, investment, new ventures, mergers and acquisitions or restructuring and reorganisation, emotions are running high. You'll be leading and navigating an emotionally charged organisation with emotionally charged teams.

Having the right strategy in place is critical. What's also critical is being sure about how you as a leader will behave and how you'll progress through this journey and take everyone else with you. At this stage, your visibility significantly reduces yet you become increasingly visible (see PRINCIPLE 7). You'll need to tap into your resilience now more than ever. You're approaching the pinnacle, preparing to leave the third or fourth camp and make the pivotal decision to attempt the summit. Knowing when to start your ascent is crucial but it's equally important to realise when you need to pivot for an even greater impact later on.

Education has always played a special role in my life. So when an opportunity came along to work with the Multi-Academy Trust in the UK, I was very excited. I was told throughout the procurement process that the last step involved a 30-minute call with the CEO, which is perfectly normal in my work. It appeared to be a formality for being involved in an innovative cultural transformation project. However, 15 minutes into my initial proposal presentation, the CEO, Neil, stopped me. 'Not a good sign,' was my first thought. But then, Neil, in his true style that I've come to know well, said, 'I like it and I want to elevate the project at Trust level. I want all the heads, all the leaders and all the schools to benefit equally.'

This resulted in an ongoing cultural transformation focused on Trust-wide collaboration. Neil has a truly open mindset and an exceptional ability to see the bigger picture. He also has a personal quality that makes him, in my opinion, one of the most transformational leaders in education. Yes, he has some unconventional ideas and he runs a very tight ship but equally he's committed to investing in his staff and leadership. For example, all of them have engaged in an innovative leadership inner circles programme so that they can take their own leadership and that of others to the next level in order to facilitate cultural change and operate in a truly collaborative fashion.

You must be able to lead yourself well before you lead others and that has never been more critical than when leading change and transformation. Amid the uncertainty, crisis and emotional charge, the market doesn't stop. Business goes on as usual. The organisation continues to run during transformation. This is your opportunity to demonstrate the calibre of your high-performance leadership by proceeding to that summit, consistently and steadily, with every step. This is also your opportunity to create high-performing teams.

Looking ahead, you're likely to secure your next role based on the success or the outcome of organisational transformation and the changes you're making. Never forget that every transformation is a cultural one. And the common denominator in transformation is you, the leader. You have to get that right. This is what you were recruited for and it's the most significant value-added contribution you can make to any organisation you work for. If there's one strategic aspect that can make the biggest difference to your success, it's leading change and transformation.

Thinking differently about transformation

Transformation is a frequently discussed topic and there are endless strategies and training programmes available to you. While learning about different strategies is important, you must be mindful and consider what will actually give you marginal gains in order to deliver success. It's often said that in today's business environment, companies can't settle for incremental improvement; they must periodically undergo performance transformations to get, and stay, on top. Yet in the volumes of pages on how to go about implementing a transformation, surprisingly little addresses the role of one important person.

Leaders with the insight to identify exemplary individuals and showcase their success stories have the power to ignite a culture of growth and achievement. You could use strategies like those of Ravi Kant. As the managing director of Tata Motors, he understood the transformative impact of highlighting the accomplishments of talented and determined individuals.

In his insightful interview on leading change, he recounts the story of a young man whose remarkable achievements on a challenging project not only propelled his own growth but also served as a powerful example to his colleagues (Kumra 2007). Through this deliberate highlighting of talent and determination, Kant demonstrated that rising through the hierarchy is attainable for those who possess the necessary skills and unwavering determination.

Kant not only inspired his colleagues but also provided a clear roadmap for others to follow. As a leader, you should recognise and celebrate the achievements of those who exemplify success, inspire others to reach greater heights and create a culture where potential is nurtured and rewarded. It's worth heeding the advice of Joseph M Tucci, CEO of EMC, who said, 'Every move you make, everything you say, is visible to all. Therefore the best approach is to lead by example.'

Transformation and change are the lifeblood of progress and growth. Senior leaders are responsible for navigating tumultuous waters and steering their teams towards success.

Leadership strategies for transformation success

Creating a compelling vision: At the heart of any successful transformation lies a compelling vision that captures the hearts and minds of your team. It's your duty as a leader to craft a vivid and inspiring narrative that paints a picture of the desired future state of your organisation – a vision that's communicated with passion and clarity and answers the fundamental question 'Where are we headed and why does it matter?' With a compelling vision, you can ignite the fires of motivation and rally your team members around a shared purpose.

Building a coalition of change agents: You can't accomplish transformation alone. You need to build a coalition of change agents to champion and drive the initiative at all levels of the organisation. These change agents, handpicked for their influence and commitment, are the torchbearers who will inspire others to embrace the transformation journey, just as Neil did in his organisation through DISC profiling, investing in his leaders through participating in leadership inner circles, which are best described as group coaching sessions that reap the benefit of collaborative intelligence and growth.

Communicating openly and transparently: In times of transformation and change, effective communication is paramount. As a leader, your role is to create a culture of open and transparent communication, ensuring that team members understand the reasons behind the change and its desired outcomes. This type of communication dispels fear, minimises resistance and avoids misinformation, enabling individuals to make sense of the changes and embrace their role in the transformation process.

In the midst of IBM's ground-breaking shift towards AI and cloud computing, CEO Ginni Rometty took centre stage, captivating her audience with her transparency. Through company-wide messages and town hall meetings, Rometty fearlessly unveiled the strategic reasoning behind this transformative journey, breaking down complex concepts, demolishing walls of uncertainty and shining a spotlight on the path ahead. It was almost as if she was handing each employee a crystal-clear roadmap, guiding them towards a shared destiny. Ultimately, Rometty's transparent communication became the secret ingredient that sparked a revolution within IBM.

Empowering and engaging employees: To drive successful change implementation, you have to empower and engage employees. By providing the necessary resources, training and authority, you're enabling your team members to actively contribute to the transformation effort. Creating a culture that values collaboration, risk taking and continual learning cultivates an environment where employees feel empowered to innovate and drive change.

Zappos, renowned for its exceptional customer service, embraced empowerment during its transition to a holacracy system. Senior leaders entrusted employees with decision-making authority, encouraging them to take ownership of their work and contribute to the company's success. This empowerment led to heightened employee engagement, increased innovation and an unparalleled customer-centric culture.

Embracing agility and iteration: Successful transformation journeys are rarely linear. Consequently you'll need to embrace agility and iteration by adjusting your strategies based on feedback and new information. Encouraging experimentation and creating a safe space for calculated risks fosters a culture of agility, enabling you to navigate uncertainty and seize emerging opportunities.

As a high-performance leader, you have the unique opportunity to lead transformation and change, forging a path towards organisational success and growth. By embracing a compelling vision, building a coalition of change agents, communicating openly, empowering employees and embracing agility, you can navigate the challenges of transformation and inspire your teams to achieve greatness. Remember, change is not to be feared but embraced as a catalyst for progress.

Observations

I'm sure you agree that organisations must continuously adapt and transform to stay competitive. When you can facilitate transformation, you're better positioned to guide your teams and organisations through these dynamic challenges. At the same time, you're positioning yourself well for career success and leaving a lasting legacy while creating more leaders. Transformation unlocks the door to sustainable success and propels organisations to new heights.

I'm often asked, 'What's the secret of sustainable success?' My reply is, 'The secret is you and your leadership in these critical times.' A recent article in *Harvard Business Review* stated that 'Disruption used to be an exceptional event that hit an unlucky few companies – think of the likes of Kodak, Polaroid and Blackberry. But in today's complex and uncertain world, as we face challenges ranging from climate change to digitisation, geopolitics to DEI [diversity, equity and inclusion], organisations must treat transformation as a core capability to master as opposed to a one-off event.' (White et al 2023)

In 1995, change management expert Professor John Kotter stated that approximately 70 per cent of transformations fail, and that holds true today. We know that the ones that do succeed have something in common and this is in line with what I've observed in high-performing leaders over the years.

Observation #1: They focus on managing the emotional journey

I find change exciting and relish the prospect. I'm sure you feel the same. However, we must be mindful of the fact that many people don't like change, transformation or crisis. When you dig deeper, you start to see that what creates that initial dislike is our relationship with uncertainty and change. Start by looking at the DISC profiles of the people around you. Those with S and C as their drivers, which represent the majority of the population, will have an adverse and fearful relationship to change. Some view it with a sense of guilt, feeling that they've done something wrong or failed, hence some team members can be extremely reluctant to join the journey. Every transformation is cultural. At this stage you might find it helpful to refer back to PRINCIPLE 7, where the DISC framework was introduced and can provide you with more detail.

Understanding the internal emotional journey that individuals typically experience when dealing with change will significantly increase the likelihood of your transformation project. Recognising that change often stirs feelings of uncertainty, fear and resistance in people, you can tailor your approach to address these emotions effectively. By acknowledging these reactions and empathising with your team members or stakeholders, you can create a supportive and understanding environment. The Kübler-Ross curve is a model developed by Elisabeth Kübler-Ross (1969). It outlines the emotional journey that individuals often experience when confronted with a significant change. The framework describes an emotional response ranging from shock and denial, through frustration and depression to eventually experiment, decision and integration. I would like to highlight a few points to focus on that leaders often neglect when using the framework.

First of all, you need to identify where you, your leadership team and everyone else involved currently are on the change curve. After the initial 'shock' of being confronted with a change, people often resist engaging with it, almost as if they're trying to prove that the change is either unreal or unnecessary. This 'denial' phase can be characterised by a burst of additional energy. There then comes a point at which those experiencing the change can no longer avoid engaging with it. At this point, denial often gives way to frustration and even depression.

It's essential not to overlook the fact that some team members might already be at the decision, integration or experimentation stage in the transformation process, possibly even ahead of you. Embrace their progress and don't hold them back. Instead, leverage their momentum to propel the transformation forward.

The right strategy for each stage of the curve is crucial. For example, if some people are in the early stages of shock, denial and frustration, don't try to start motivating them, because this will have the opposite effect. You'll demotivate them and, as a result, they'll switch off. The best approach is to first ensure creative alignment and only then to maximise communication, which includes listening and not necessarily just talking at them. Eventually, a point will be reached where they start to engage with the idea of change and this is the critical point where the curve starts to climb. Only then do you start motivating.

Using the DISC framework, outlined in PRINCIPLE 7, will further help you to understand how different personalities respond to change. People with a D in their profile who are achievement driven and love change will race through it. Those with the C, who are more detailed and systematic, and those with the S, who are consensus driven and team orientated, will be slower to respond and can outwardly appear resistant. People with the I will be excited but may not proceed as quickly. Your biggest opportunity lies in the quiet middle, because if you don't tap into them, there is a risk that they'll tap into the people who are more resistant to change and then you'll have a bigger challenge to deal with.

Don't forget there will be people in your team who'll listen to every word you say and are already working ahead of you. Don't lose them. Understanding the emotional journey people go through can make the difference between success and failure in transformational change projects. It's often not a strategy failure but a failure of leaders to take people with them.

Leadership expert John Maxwell's '25-50-25' principle of change (2019) can help you decide where to focus and who you take with you. One of the biggest mistakes leaders make is spending too much time on the people who are reluctant to come on the journey.

+ Understand that the 25 per cent who resist aren't going to change. The greatest leader in the world couldn't get them to change their minds. Accept it.

+ Understand you can't make that 25 per cent happy and that trying to appease them only encourages them to continue resisting!

+ Create opportunities for the middle 50 per cent to spend time with the top 25 per cent, because attitudes are contagious.

+ Ask the 25 per cent who support your efforts to influence the 50 per cent and give them credibility and a platform. They'll help you help the organisation move forward.

Leading transformations features throughout all my work and is often the topic that comes up in conference breaks at the coffee machine. So when I spotted Emily, a former client, at an event where I was speaking, I couldn't resist asking her about how her recent transformation project had gone. Seen as a talented and visionary leader, she was tasked with leading a major organisational transformation. Aware of the emotional roller coaster that accompanies change, Emily told me that she drew her inspiration from the Kübler-Ross model, which we had covered during our coaching session a while ago. It has helped her by openly acknowledging the apprehension and resistance that arise during times of transformation. She created a safe and supportive environment where employees could express their concerns, frustrations and fears without judgement.

But she didn't doesn't stop there. She also embraced the 25-50-25 principle, recognising that not everyone adapts to change at the same pace. She understood that approximately 25 per cent of her team would be early adopters, embracing the transformation with enthusiasm. These individuals became her champions and ambassadors of change, spreading positive energy and inspiring others to join in. She focused her attention on engaging with this group, leveraging their influence and passion to create momentum. She empowered them with additional responsibilities, recognising their commitment and allowing them to drive the transformation forward.

Emily then devoted her energy to the middle 50 per cent, the majority who may be uncertain or even sceptical about the change. By patiently addressing their questions, she gradually brought them on board and helped them overcome resistance. She understood that around 25 per cent of her team might initially struggle to accept the transformation. They may resist the change, feeling overwhelmed or disconnected from the new direction.

She used the Kübler-Ross model and the 25-50-25 principle as guiding frameworks, recognising and honouring the emotional dynamics of transformation, which she has seen as the ultimate key to her project's success.

Observation #2: They embrace the 5+1 Model

Coaching and training many senior leaders worldwide has inspired me to subtract complexity from how to lead with resilience through transformation, uncertainty and crisis. As I highlighted in PRINCIPLE 3, for high performers mental resilience is a powerful source of competitive advantage. It's not about being tough and emotionless but about your mental capacity to quickly turn things around and recover confidently, moving forward as fast as possible. As has been said, 'Leadership is not about staying comfortable; it's about pushing the boundaries, taking risks and leading the charge in transformational journeys.'

My 5+1 Model is based on my many conversations with leaders and their organisations and offers a highly practical approach, whether you're leading change or transformation or simply wishing to navigate uncertainty and crisis with confidence and resilience. It originated at the end of a senior leadership transformation course when a participant caught me at the end of the session. He asked me for some performance hacks for leading transformation. So I got out the flip chart and wrote out 1, 2, 3, 4, 5 and then drew a line below and added +1.

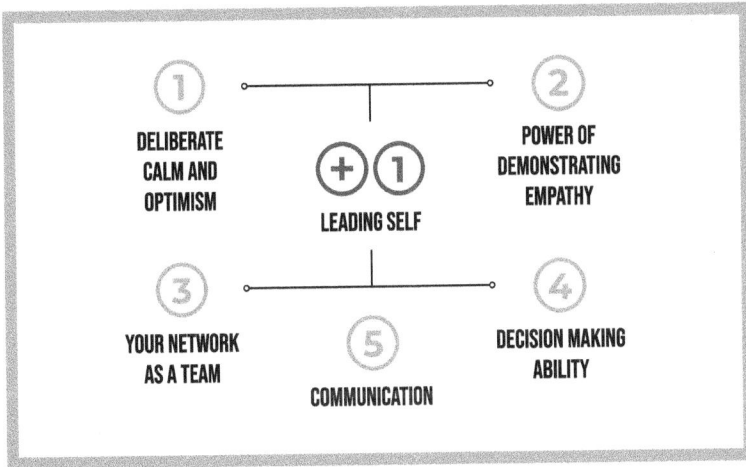

Figure 9: The 5+1 Model

Why not six? I understand that self-kindness might not be the first thing that comes to mind when you think of leadership or transformation. However, I want to emphasise its significance. Take a moment to reflect on this important aspect. Begin with +1, leading yourself, and everything else will follow from there.

+1 Leading self

If we can't lead ourselves, it's challenging to lead others. Working with high-performing leaders, it's crucial to highlight it. Whether you like it or not, you'll make mistakes. I strongly encourage you to be kind to yourself and exercise self-compassion and gratitude. The learning curve is steep for all involved, filled with uncertainty and change, so I appreciate it.

1. Deliberate calm and optimism

The key word here is deliberate because no leader will always be calm and optimistic during a crisis or uncertainty. Therefore choosing a calm and optimistic mindset requires a conscious effort and tapping into your emotional intelligence. So focus on what matters and prioritise with confidence.

2. Power of demonstrating empathy

Empathy is like gratitude; it's best when demonstrated. Therefore you must consciously consider how you'll show empathy to your audience. At this point, it's essential to differentiate between the different types of empathy: cognitive, emotional and compassionate. I'd encourage you to prioritise cognitive empathy, otherwise your energy bank will soon be empty if you go on everyone's emotional journey.

3. Your network as a team

The higher you go, the lonelier it gets. This is especially true when you're leading change or transformation. So make your network your team! Share and engage with peers from your organisation or other industries. I don't doubt that you'll find many of your peers are facing similar challenges. It's for this very reason that I run leadership inner circles and mastermind groups.

4. Decision-making ability

Your decision-making ability will be crucial to success. You'll need to be clear about your decision goal, then visualise the process as 'crossing the road': pause, assess, anticipate and go. You won't always get all your decisions right but time is critical, so assess the risk and go.

5. Communication, communication and communication

I've seen many otherwise well-planned transformations fail at effective communication. Of course, at no point will you have all the information, nor can you share all the information with everyone. However, I can confidently ensure you'll be ahead of the game if you focus on two aspects. First, transparency and frequency mean you don't have to wait until you have something significant to announce. Second, your 'best friend' will be micro-communication that keeps everyone informed and in the zone of psychological safety.

I have to say that ever since the model came into existence, it has proved to be my most photographed and requested slide ever, both in the context of training and speaking engagements. I'm so grateful to all the leaders who have inspired me to devise the model and of course those who initially asked the question at that training session in 2018. Before you read further, I want you to reflect on the model and start with +1 because you are the biggest marginal gain of any transformation project.

Observation #3: They don't lose sight of the bigger picture

The ability to lead transformation is an essential skill that will allow you to drive organisational growth, adapt to changing environments and stay ahead of the competition. It's crucial for ensuring your long-term career success as a high-performing leader. When you're leading a large and complex project with many stakeholders and team members involved, it's easy to lose sight of the ultimate goal. Why do organisations need to transform, especially when the process itself often involves restructuring? The purpose of the transformation is your biggest opportunity to connect with everyone involved. So, to keep focused on the bigger picture, start with the 'why'. By constantly reminding yourself and all involved of this vision, you'll ensure that everyone is aligned and working towards a common purpose. This alignment fosters cohesion, cooperation and a sense of shared direction, which you'll need along the way.

Here's the bigger picture of transformation:

Adapting to changing markets: Markets are constantly evolving, driven by technological advancements, shifting consumer preferences and global trends, and as the leader you need the ability and agility to adapt your organisation to these changes.

Embracing innovation: Transformation often requires embracing innovation and nurturing a culture of creativity within the organisation. You must be able to encourage and support innovative thinking that can drive breakthrough solutions and stay ahead of the competition.

Responding to disruptive technologies: Disruptive technologies can reshape entire industries. Recognising and understanding the potential of these technologies enables you to lead transformation in a way that positions your organisation as a pioneer in this new landscape.

Engaging and inspiring employees: To lead transformation you need to be able to engage and inspire employees throughout the change process. This entails communicating the vision, rallying the team and building a culture of trust and resilience.

Driving organisational growth: Transformation often involves expanding into new markets, diversifying product offerings or implementing strategic initiatives to drive growth. In leading transformation, you'll need to navigate these expansion opportunities and position your organisation for sustainable success.

Managing change and overcoming resistance: Successfully leading transformation depends on your ability to effectively manage change and overcome resistance within the organisation to minimise disruption and engage stakeholders.

While focusing on the big picture in the midst of what often looks like chaos and taking others with you on the journey isn't an easy task, it's highly rewarding when you nail it.

In the world of sports, few transformational leaders can match the electrifying impact of Jürgen Klopp, the charismatic manager of Liverpool Football Club. Klopp's journey with Liverpool is a testament to the power of focusing on the big picture while leading a team through a remarkable transformation. When Klopp arrived at Liverpool in 2015, the club was longing for a return to its glory days. With resolute determination, Klopp set his sights on transforming Liverpool into a formidable force, not just in England but on the grandest stages of European football.

From the very beginning, Klopp painted a vivid picture of success for his players, staff and loyal fans. He infused the club with a contagious belief that they could conquer any challenge, overcome any obstacle and lift prestigious trophies once again. The big picture was crystal clear: Liverpool would rise to the pinnacle of the footballing world. Amid trials and tribulations, Klopp never lost sight of that big picture. He implemented a dynamic and high-intensity playing style, demanding unfaltering commitment and a relentless work ethic from his squad. Klopp's passion and charisma were infectious, igniting a fire within his players and inspiring them to push beyond their limits.

Even during tough times, when defeats and setbacks threatened to derail the transformation, Klopp's unyielding belief in the big picture remained unshaken. He rallied his troops, urging them to stay focused, reminding them that greatness is achieved through perseverance, unity and unwavering faith in the vision they shared.

The transformational journey bore its fruits in the unforgettable 2018–19 season when Liverpool clinched the UEFA Champions League title, signalling a triumphant return to the summit of European football. But Klopp's appetite for success didn't stop there. In the following season, Liverpool secured the English Premier League title, breaking a three-decade-long drought and etching their names in footballing history.

Klopp's ability to keep the big picture in sharp focus, his infectious enthusiasm and total belief in his team's potential electrified Anfield, Liverpool's legendary stadium. Under his guidance, Liverpool evolved into a powerhouse, captivating fans worldwide with their thrilling brand of football and conquering the hearts of football enthusiasts everywhere.

Klopp's leadership journey at Liverpool serves as a powerful reminder of the incredible outcomes that can be achieved when you embrace the big picture. Klopp transformed Liverpool into a formidable force, etching his name in the annals of footballing greatness.

This is why I say never lose sight of the purpose. Every transformation is about cultural change, so you need to take people with you. And if you're not reminding yourself and others of what the purpose is in all this, you can easily become lost and jeopardise the success of the project. It can be difficult to do this continually, which is when your coach, your mentor, your team members and your peers come into play, reminding you occasionally why the restructuring has to happen, particularly when there appears to be a mismatch – for example, when redundancies are involved.

The purpose isn't the restructuring, and it certainly isn't what appears in the headlines that the organisation has let 500 workers go. That's the outcome. So what is the purpose behind it? It could be efficiency, it could be market changes. Organisations often need to restructure for long-term sustainability. The key to your success in leading transformation is keeping the purpose and bigger picture front and centre of your mind as you lead your organisation through this journey.

REFLECT AND GROW

Here are the top three key takeaways from PRINCIPLE 12:

+ *As a leader, change, transformation and leading in uncertainty and crisis will be the key catalysts in your leadership and career success. And the secret to successful change and transformation is you and your leadership.*

+ *Focus on managing and navigating the emotional journey.*

+ *Embrace the 5+1 Model and don't lose sight of the big picture.*

Reflect on the three points below:

+ *What have been the most successful change and transformation initiatives you have led?*

+ *Do you find leading in uncertainty challenging or a source of motivation and excitement?*

+ *Take the 5+1 Model and share it with other leaders. Try it out yourself and see the difference it makes, not just to you but to others around you as well as the outcome of the project.*

YOUR PERFORMANCE ADVANTAGE HACK

Take five minutes to revisit some of the strategies for successful transformation. Choose one and consider how you will strengthen this capacity.

FINAL REFLECTIONS

Dearest reader,

Congratulations on positioning yourself for success and taking your leadership and career to the next level. As a high-performance thinker, you know that your long-term success is not a matter of luck but a result of your conscious and continual efforts.

I want to express my sincere gratitude for placing your trust in me and joining me on the journey through the 12 PRINCIPLES and tapping into your performance advantage. Whether you've immersed yourself in the entirety of this book or selectively focused on specific parts, your commitment to personal growth is inspiring. Your devotion to your professional advancement reflects your dedication, exceptional character and ambitious drive.

As you reach the end of this book, you may find yourself feeling overwhelmed, with many ideas swirling in your mind, wondering where to begin. Take a moment to recall your initial expectations after reading the introduction.

+ What were your thoughts at that time?
+ How has your perspective evolved or shifted since then?
+ Which principles do you intend to prioritise in the upcoming six months?

Don't just put this book on the shelf or store it in your digital library. Instead, use the 12 PRINCIPLES and observations as your go-to guiding companion whenever you're ready to elevate your leadership and career to the next level. Return to its teachings: embrace the power of your high-performance thinking, rely on your leadership superpower, tap into your resilience and subtract complexity to add value. You know that this works!

I encourage you to keep your leadership journey easily accessible and leverage your acquired self-leadership strategies. Continuously refine and adapt them to suit your needs. Remember, you're in complete control of your leadership path. Remain mindful of the impact of your communication, never take it for granted and always be aware of your visibility. Leadership is a profound responsibility and your actions are a testament to your character. See change and mistakes as opportunities. Embrace the power of unlearning, allowing yourself to relearn, grow and maintain your relevance in the years to come.

I have a genuine passion for my work, so I can understand why you may be tempted to invest significant energy into your job. However, remember that focusing solely on your job is insufficient for building sustainable long-term career success. As you navigate your professional journey, ensure that your personal branding remains relevant to your envisioned destination. Never underestimate the importance of mastering the art of influencing, as it will play a pivotal role in your leadership endeavours. You'll undoubtedly encounter opportunities to lead transformative initiatives, navigate uncertainty and manage crises. In preparation for these challenges, I urge you to keep a copy of my 5+1 Model as a valuable resource. Revisit it regularly, share it with trusted individuals in your network, and remember to commence with the +1 because there's no leadership without you.

'There you go,' as my grandparents would lovingly say whenever I presented them with yet another complex challenge I intended to solve. This time, however, I am 50. I decided to capture decades of professional experience and many years of encounters within the pages of this book, blending expertise with inspiration into 12 PRINCIPLES for high-performance leaders. What challenge will you set for yourself next? How will you utilise the powerful perspective you've gained on the power of high-performance thinking, the significance of your leadership journey and career success?

I don't see leadership as a heroic act that takes place in isolation. By going on a journey with others, you'll grow faster, go further and create more leaders. Therefore I've never been a fan of the term 'self-made'. I've been inspired by many along the way and supported and encouraged by many more. If you've read this book, you know who you are; however, some of you can no longer see this, while others perhaps never realised that they were a source of energy.

Before writing THE PERFORMANCE ADVANTAGE, I asked myself what impact I wanted to have on you, the reader, as I extended my invitation in the introduction for your utmost trust, and we embarked on this transformative journey together.

I wanted you to think differently about high performance, your leadership and your career and recognise the transformative power of the marginal gains the 12 PRINCIPLES will give you to take you to the next level so that you can further foster a profound sense of focus, empowerment and success.

I aimed to provide you with essential tools, practical insights and a comprehensive understanding of what it takes to fulfil your leadership potential.

Above all, I intended to inspire you to share this book's invaluable knowledge with others. Because ultimately, true leaders are catalysts in cultivating and nurturing future leaders.

I continue to encourage you to stay in your own high-performance lane and focus your attention on your own game. However, I also invite you to challenge yourself and others, both consciously and continually. If you do this, you'll create a powerful synergy that fosters an environment of growth and success. Embrace the journey and make every step count towards striving for excellence. Your dedication and commitment will not only lead to your own success but also inspire those around you to achieve greatness.

Never be complacent with your current level of performance. Treat every day as an opportunity to become a better version of yourself, both personally and professionally. Keep setting higher standards, pushing boundaries and stretching your capabilities. As you embark on this journey of challenge and growth, stay humble. Recognise that there's always more to learn and that you can draw inspiration from others. Seek out role models and the right performance coach who can guide you on your path.

I pledge to continue my life quest of making high-performance leaders, teams and organisations think differently so they can succeed at their next level. I shall embrace the 12 PRINCIPLES myself and promise not to stop here but to grow and maximise the opportunities ahead. I'm immensely proud to be your companion on your leadership success journey towards becoming the leader you deserve to be.

Till next time, with gratitude and unwavering curiosity,

Agnes

RESOURCES

Adams G S, Converse B A et al (2021) 'People systematically overlook subtractive changes.' *Nature* 7 April. URL: nature.com/articles/s41586-021-03380-y

Bennis, W (2009) *On Becoming a Leader*. Basic Books.

Brown, B (2012) *Daring Greatly: How the courage to be vulnerable transforms the way we live, love, parent, and lead*. Avery.

Brown, B (2017) *Braving the Wilderness: The quest for true belonging and the courage to stand alone*. Random House.

Buckingham, M (2019) '3 proven ways to win at work.' CNBC 14 January. URL: cnbc.com/2019/01/14/marcus-buckingham-3-scientifically-proven-ways-to-win-at-work.html

Clear, J (2018) *Atomic Habits: Tiny changes, remarkable results: an easy & proven way to build good habits & break bad ones*. Penguin Random House.

Goldsmith, M (2008) *What Got You Here Won't Get You There*. Profile Books.

Goleman, D (2018) 'Do you make this one big mistake about emotional intelligence?' LinkedIn 1 March. URL: linkedin.com/pulse/do-you-make-one-big-mistake-emotional-intelligence-daniel-goleman

Hallenbeck, G (2016) *Lead 4 Success: Learn the essentials of true leadership*. Center for Creative Leadership.

Hu, J, Zhang, S et al (2022) 'When leaders heed the lessons of mistakes: Linking leaders' recall of learning from mistakes to expressed humility.' *Personnel Psychology* 27 December. URL: onlinelibrary.wiley.com/doi/10.1111/peps.12570

Kelly, S (2019) 'Microsoft: What went right under Satya Nadella?' BBC2, 2 February. URL: bbc.com/news/technology-47078013

Kübler-Ross, E (1969) *On Death & Dying.* Scribner.

Kumra, G (2007) 'Leading change: An interview with the managing director of Tata Motors'. URL: mckinsey.com/capabilities/people-and-organizational-performance/our-insights/leading-change-an-interview-with-the-managing-director-of-tata-motors

Manz, C C (1983) *The Art of Self-leadership: Strategies for personal effectiveness in your life and work.* Prentice-Hall.

Marston, W M (1928) *Emotions of Normal People.* Harcourt.

Maxwell, J J (2019) 'The 25-50-25 principle of change'. URL: johnmaxwell.com/blog/the-25-50-25-principle-of-change/

Mendelow, A (1991) 'Stakeholder mapping'. *Proceedings of the 2nd International Conference on Information Systems* 5(2).

O'Reilly, B (2018) *Unlearn: Let go of past success to achieve extraordinary.* McGraw Hill.

Ong, S A (2022) *Energize: Make the most of every moment.* Penguin Business.

Rath, T (2007) *StrengthsFinder 2.0.* Gallup Press.

Riopel, L (2019) 'Resilience examples: What key skills make you resilient?' *Positive Psychology* 20 January. URL: positivepsychology.com/resilience-skills/#resilience-types

Sandberg, S (2013) *Lean In: Women, work, and the will to lead.* Knopf.

Schwartz, B (2004) *The Paradox of Choice.* Harper Perennial.

Simon, H (1955) 'A behavioral model of rational choice'. *The Quarterly Journal of Economics* 69(1).

Sinek, S (2014) *Leaders Eat Last: Why some teams pull together and others don't.* Portfolio.

Syed, M (2016) *Black Box Thinking: Marginal gains and the secrets of high performance.* John Murray.

White A, Wheelock M et al (2023) '6 key levers of a successful organizational transformation'. *Harvard Business Review* 10 May. URL: hbr.org/2023/05/6-key-levers-of-a-successful-organizational-transformation

Young, R (2021) *Simplify: A high performance playbook to win the real game.* Richard Young Consulting Limited.

ACKNOWLEDGEMENTS

Writing this book has been an exceptional journey, made possible by the significant contributions of many individuals who supported this project.

I extend my heartfelt appreciation to the numerous global leaders whose narratives form the backbone of this work. Your transparency and willingness to share your insights and experiences provide invaluable lessons for fellow high-performance leaders.

I'm grateful to my colleagues within the leadership community. Your varied experiences and broad perspectives have enriched the content of this book, deepening its impact.

I would also like to acknowledge my wider professional network. Your diverse encounters and insightful feedback have significantly broadened not just the scope of this book but also my understanding of leadership.

I owe a special note of gratitude to The Right Book Press team, specifically Sue, Bev, Andrew and Paul, for your expertise and support. Your dedication and commitment have been instrumental in shaping this work into its final form.

To my family and friends, your ongoing understanding, love and support have provided a consistent source of strength throughout the demanding periods of writing and research. Your faith in this project and in me has been immensely encouraging.

Alison Coleman, the journey would not have been the same without you.

Finally, to you, the reader – thank you for your interest and for investing your time in this book. I'm confident that the stories and insights contained within these pages will resonate with you and take you to the next level on your own high-performance leadership journey.

EU Safety Representative: euComply OÜ Pärnu mnt 139b-14 11317 Tallinn
Estonia hello@eucompliancepartner.com +33 756 90241

www.ingramcontent.com/pod-product-compliance
Lightning Source LLC
Chambersburg PA
CBHW041145230326
41599CB00039BA/7187